How to Write
Better Résumés

SECOND EDITION

by

Adele Lewis

President, Career Blazers Agency, Inc.
New York City

BARRON'S EDUCATIONAL SERIES, INC.

New York • London • Toronto • Sydney

All inquiries should be addressed to:
Barron's Educational Series, Inc.
250 Wireless Boulevard
Hauppauge, New York 11788

Library of Congress Catalog Card No. 82-181-66

International Standard Book No. 0-8120-2372-2

Library of Congress Cataloging in Publication Data

Lewis, Adele Beatrice, 1927-
   How to write better résumés.

   Bibliography: p. vi
   1. Résumés (Employment)   I. Title.
HF5383.L48   1982   650.1'4   82-18166
ISBN 0-8120-2372-2

PRINTED IN THE UNITED STATES OF AMERICA
7   100   13 12

Contents

Introduction

As business becomes more complex and sophisticated, so does the procedure of recruiting and job hunting. There was a time when job seekers could simply visit a personnel department and be interviewed, but that time has long since passed.

Employers and personnel departments all over the country report that résumés have become the most effective way of screening candidates to determine who will be interviewed. Résumés are expected of candidates at every level — executives, accountants, attorneys, secretaries, nurses, teachers, editors, publicists, trainees, etc.

These same employers also indicate that of the thousands of résumés they receive daily, only a very few impress them enough to consider their writers as serious job candidates.

It is the purpose of this book to show you, in a logical step-by-step procedure, exactly how to write a superior résumé — one which will strengthen your job campaign and ultimately get you the very job you want.

I wish to thank all our clients, both job seekers and recruiters, who were so generous with their time and their suggestions. I am very grateful to my son William Lewis, President of Career Blazers Personnel Services, Inc., for his continual support, and for keeping me supplied with an excellent staff of researchers and manuscript typists. And, lastly, special thanks to my editor, Ruth Pecan, for her guidance along the way.

Selected Bibliography of Job Reference Books

DICTIONARY OF OCCUPATIONAL TITLES
2 Volumes and supplement
Published by U.S. Department of Labor, Washington, D.C.

A definitive survey of all occupations and jobs currently held in the United States at this time. Descriptions of the education and skills required for each job category are useful additions to your information about the job market.

ESTIMATE OF WORKER TRAIT REQUIREMENTS FOR 4000 JOBS AS DEFINED IN THE DICTIONARY OF OCCUPATIONAL TITLES
Published by U.S. Department of Labor, Washington, D.C.

An informative book that thoroughly discusses the aptitude necessary for specific job categories. It also specifies working conditions and training time.

MOODY'S INDUSTRIAL MANUAL
Published by Moody's Investment Service
99 Church Street, New York, New York 10017

A useful directory that lists major corporations and provides such information as the nature of its business, address and name of each corporate officer. This volume gives information you should know about a specific company before being interviewed.

OCCUPATIONAL OUTLOOK HANDBOOK
Published by U.S. Department of Labor, Washington, D.C.

A comprehensive career guidance book that describes hundreds of occupations. It also includes information on working conditions, places of employment, training and education needed, earnings, and expected job prospects for each occupation.

POOR'S REGISTER OF CORPORATION DIRECTORS AND EXECUTIVES
Published by Standard and Poor's Corporation
345 Hudson Station, New York, New York 10014

A complete directory of major corporations. It provides the name and address of each corporation and lists the name of the executive. An excellent source of information when preparing an individual, direct mail campaign.

Finding the Right Job

Job hunting can be either a catastrophe or a triumph. It can plummet you into the depths of depression or lift you to the summit of self-confidence. From long experience in dealing with a variety of job seekers, I've come to the conclusion that looking for and getting a job is a skill. It is a skill that anyone can learn easily, and perhaps for that reason it is too often disregarded or discarded. Like any skill, it requires some training, careful analysis, and huge amounts of determination and perseverence before it can be executed successfully. If you are armed with the right tools for job hunting, finding your "place in the sun" can be an exciting as well as a rewarding experience.

In looking for a job, you should always *aim* for the best available, and try to avoid settling for less. But you must maintain an open and realistic attitude, evaluating each opportunity with a flexible and farsighted view. Even if, at the outset, you don't find the "perfect" job, the one you do get may be the first step of your climb to success.

While I believe in trying to hold out for the very best, I am also aware that a job is often what you make of it. It is not unusual to hear that one of my firm's recent placements who took a secretarial position has been moved up to an important managerial spot. Reports about mailroom clerks becoming researchers, buyers becoming production managers, or sales personnel becoming executives are not uncommon. Draftsmen soon head design departments; copy boys' names appear in by-lines. Remember that the most exciting jobs are usually filled by people who are already in the office or on the floor.

Are Jobs Available?

One of the most important attributes a job seeker must have is a realistic and optimistic point of view. You must realize that, whether the economy is booming or sluggish, there are always job openings. Companies are forever recruiting. Some people retire, others are promoted, managers and executives are transferred, and, in consequence, staff vacancies are created. Usually someone must be hired to fill them. No matter what economic conditions may be, someone is always trying to hire someone else. Were this not so, employment agencies would have to close their doors; on the contrary, more than 5,000 agencies in the United States are currently interviewing applicants and getting job specifications from personnel directors. And they support themselves by the fees they get for matching applicants to the job "specs."

In times of economic recession, beginners might have to hunt a little longer for jobs, liberal arts graduates may have to settle temporarily for lesser goals, and the "phased outs" might have to change fields or even relocate; but if each person is looking seriously for work and puts forth sincere effort, more than adequate compensation will result from the effort. Often, the outcome of a successful job campaign (even in "hard times") is several job offers, and the problem changes from "how to find a job" to "which one shall I accept?"

It is my belief that you should take the job where you'll be happiest. Every job has its psychological fringe benefits, and these, in the long run, can more than counterbalance what might be a slight initial salary deficiency. If you are happy in a job, you will do good work (and conversely, if you do good work, you'll be happy) and rapidly receive tangible recognition. In addition, contentment in your work will spill over into other areas of your life and is, therefore, an important and vital job asset.

The Positive Side of Adversity

Right now, there is an extreme shortage of job seekers in certain areas. Can you believe that, at this point — several years after the onset of the 1969 recession — personnel people all over the country are reporting terrible shortages of qualified job applicants with two to twelve years of experience? Although everybody is now aware, as a result of all the publicity in the press, of the extent of the unemployment problem in our country, only the people in a position to hire are conscious of the difficulties in recruiting personnel today.

At the moment, employment agencies are complaining more about the lack of job seekers than of job orders. Companies large and small report a lack of capable applicants for any position beyond the entry level. There may be many people hunting for jobs; there are still many jobs looking for people.

The reason for this personnel shortage is that employed people are "staying put." Companies are experiencing less turnover than in the recent past, and there are no longer available on the job market employed people in search of greener pastures and willing to gamble on "trading up." Consequently the total number of experienced and qualified people who are job hunting is smaller, much smaller, than in the "go-go" years.

It might well be that the type of position you are seeking is much easier to find now than it would have been in the prosperous sixties. This is the positive aspect of a slow market. There is the pervasive feeling of a depressed economy; people who are working, therefore, are not looking for new or better job opportunities. This leaves fewer people competing for the existing jobs. As a result, in what would seem to be a tight job market, it might be far easier than you had expected to find the job you want.

Use this market to your advantage. Once you've mastered the job hunting skill, it will be a lasting asset. Given the tools for the job hunt — a superior résumé, great determination, and common sense and realistic direction, there is little doubt that you will reach your ultimate potential. Success will be almost unavoidable.

The Nitty Gritty

In the job hunt, the single most important tool is a carefully thought-out, attractively designed, well-written résumé. Whether or not an interview is granted results from the impression made by a résumé. In any personnel department, the first contact with a person as well as the impact that person may have is through a résumé.

"Résumé" — pronounced REHZ-uh-may — is from a French word meaning "summary." A résumé is not only a summary of your experience and education; it is also an advertisement selling *you*. Like any advertisement, it should be attractive, well-organized, and capable of creating interest in its product — you!

This book will teach you to write a better résumé, a résumé that will get results, that will get the interviews, and that ultimately will get you a better job.

Contents and Style

2

The Contents of a Résumé

Every résumé must *identify and describe* the writer.

You *must* include the following:

Your name, address, and telephone number
Description of your work history
Professional licenses
Publications, if any
Membership in professional organizations
Description of your educational background
Academic honors, if any

You *may* or *may not* include the items below:

Job objective or career goal
Brief personal history
Capsule description of work history
Hobby information
Willingness to travel or relocate
Military service or draft status
Statement of health
Personal data — marital status and number of children, age, height, weight

You must *never* insert the following details:

Reasons for leaving past jobs
Past salaries or present salary requirements
A photograph of yourself
Names of spouse or children
Names and addresses of references

Résumé Styles

You have several styles to choose from in writing a résumé. Although every résumé should contain a brief, concise summary of your work history and educational background, the style or approach differs in the arrangement of this data. Despite the variations that exist within each of them, basically there are five different résumé styles or approaches:

- Historical or Chronological
- Functional
- Analytical
- Synoptic/Amplified
- Imaginative, Creative, or Informal

I will discuss and evaluate each of these, giving, as well, one hypothetical résumé in each of the styles so that you can decide which would be best for you.

HISTORICAL OR CHRONOLOGICAL APPROACH

As the name implies, this style presents information in chronological succession. It is necessary, however, that the presentation be in *inverse* chronological order, starting with the present or most recent experience and moving backwards in time through each datum.

Dates are always included. They can be displayed in a vertical column set apart from the other information, put on a line before the pertinent information, or included as an integral part of each paragraph of your history. Generally, one of the first two is preferred, as most employers like to be able to determine at a glance the dates involved.

Education is treated in the same manner as your employment history. Your most advanced degree is given first, followed, in inverse order, by all other degrees and certificates. Academic honors would be included in this grouping.

If you care to include a job objective, it would be placed at the very beginning, after your name and address, but before your history. All other required or optional information should be placed at the very end.

As a rule, the chronological approach begins with your most recent experience, whether it be work or education. There are special circumstances where this rule should be broken. For instance, if you secured a college degree by working in one field and going to school nights, and are looking for work in the new field that the degree has qualified you for, you would start with your educational history (after your name and address, of course). However, had you gotten the degree for reasons of pride, but want to continue in the same field you were in prior to completing your studies, you would start the chronology with your work history. In short, give prominence to whatever is most descriptive of your talents and abilities. You want to emphasize, from the start, your most salable assets.

The chronological résumé — like any other — should be brief and consist of only one page, if possible. In no event should it exceed two pages. If you feel that your history *demands* three pages, the information you find so fascinating will probably be a complete bore to a reader of your résumé.

I feel that this style of résumé is the most effective, and I strongly recommend its use. A survey of such "résumé readers" as personnel people, office managers, and corporate executives confirms my opinion:

"... much easier to read ... " is a quote from the president of a well-known manufacturing firm.

"I can tell at a glance if the employment history fits our needs," says the general counsel of a major company listed on the stock exchange.

"... precise and to the point ... " is the opinion of the vice-president of a large music and record company.

"Not only is the expertise indicated, but we can easily see how long it's been employed," says the chairman of a national foundation.

FUNCTIONAL APPROACH

The functional résumé, as you can assume from its name, emphasizes your qualifications and abilities in terms of your job titles and responsibilities. This style of résumé highlights different areas of employment experience and is arranged with its most significant functions and responsibilities first. Each job title is followed by a brief description of duties and expertise. Dates are not given, or if included, are inconspicuous.

Education is treated in a separate area and, as with the work history, dates are omitted.

I believe, in order to make a functional résumé more effective, a concise chronological history, including dates, should be added. Even though the functional résumé is a perfect vehicle for describing actual talents and areas of achievement, the omission of dates lessens its effectiveness. A résumé without dates is a much weaker résumé and could even become a liability. Listing all dates will subtly reassure the reader that nothing has been deleted and that no periods of time have been unaccounted for deliberately or, at best, overlooked.

The body of information in this résumé is followed and concluded by your personal data.

The functional résumé is an excellent presentation for those people who have had few jobs — either executives who have been employed in one or two firms for a considerable length of time, or younger persons who, so far, have had only one job. In such cases a chronological sequence is of less interest than a thorough description of each function or responsibility.

ANALYTICAL APPROACH

The analytical résumé, like the functional, rejects an historical or chronological sequence of employment and educational history, and instead lists in a chronological sequence an analysis of each particular skill. The particular ability is the important facet in this type of résumé.

Your work history and education are fragmented into significant talents and each skill is listed separately. As these skills have been exercised, probably, in more than one position, names of employers and dates are not attached to each item.

The analytical résumé is especially useful when attempting to change career goals. If your qualifications and responsibilities are valuable in more than one field, it is more sensible to emphasize the skill by setting it apart than to bury it with less significant skills.

Like the functional résumé, the usual format for the analytical résumé omits dates. However, most résumé readers feel that a résumé loses effectiveness if dates are not shown. Dateless résumés might imply a spotty work history, involving too many job changes or time gaps that the applicant feels would be awkward to explain. Consequently, I recommend that a very concise chronological history listing all employers, job titles, schools, and dates also be included. This history should be placed right after the job objective, if it is used, or towards the end, immediately before your personal data.

SYNOPTIC / AMPLIFIED APPROACH

The synoptic/amplified résumé is the only style whose organization requires two pages. The first page would consist of your name and address, job objective, chronological history of employment and education, and personal data. The chronological history of employment would list job title and employer, clearly setting off the dates.

At the bottom of the page, in parentheses, would be the statement "Please see following for amplification." The amplification should be limited to one page, but it may be necessary to continue to a second for a total of three pages. The amplification would again list dates of employment and name of employer, as well as nature of the business and your duties and responsibilities in that company.

While this is an effective presentation, especially for a person whose duties and responsibilities went far beyond those normally seen as the functions of a given job title, it has the disadvantage of being one page longer, through its design, than other résumé styles giving the same information. In addition, in preparing the amplification, more space being available, there is a tendency for one to become long-winded and give extraneous information that is not pertinent to the résumé.

IMAGINATIVE OR CREATIVE APPROACH

A résumé can be as creative as its writer desires. There are, however, three provisos: first, it should contain all the necessary information; second, the information should be easily extracted; and third, it should not be capable of offending anyone.

If you decide to use the creative approach, keep in mind that, while it can serve as a vehicle for displaying your literary or artistic talents, it is primarily a means of communicating certain information which the résumé reader must have. You very well may be a second James Joyce, but the résumé reader cannot devote his lifetime to your résumé. Similarly, two cartoon characters giving questions and answers might convey all the information and also show your drawing ability, but, while you might make an impression for originality, your résumé might not be read to the end. Keep in mind that if you have published writings or art, you can always indicate on your résumé that you have a portfolio available. It is dangerous to be too gimmicky or too cute. Overly creative résumés might catch the eye. Nevertheless, they often fail to sustain interest, and become completely ineffectual. Most résumé readers feel that a résumé is a business matter and should be presented in a businesslike manner.

If you want to be imaginative, it is best to use some simple device that will distinguish your résumé from the dozens of others that arrive in personnel offices every day. For instance, you could use colored paper, preferably of a pale or pastel hue soft enough to allow contrast with the printed text. Purple ink on hot pink paper may catch the eye but it also will tire the sight.

Another simple device that makes a résumé stand out is to use different type faces and type sizes for the various parts of the résumé. But the same caveat applies that applies to the use of color: avoid any type that is difficult to read. Also, don't overdo it.

As a general rule, creative résumés may be appropriate to the arts, graphics, and advertising fields; but for most other businesses and the professions, it is best to employ one of the standard résumé styles.

CHRONOLOGICAL RÉSUMÉ

George Roberts	Born: 2-22-33
12 Grey Place	6′ 0″
Albuquerque, New Mexico 87116	165 lbs.
Home Phone: (505) 555-1246	Married, one child
Business Phone: (505) 555-2395	Will relocate

Work Experience

1971–present

SALES DIRECTOR
Mission Museum
Albuquerque, New Mexico 87103

Originally an unpaid volunteer, was offered full charge of sales program of local nonprofit private museum. Developed energetic program that within two years resulted in sales becoming significant source of museum's income. Opened special sales desk for young people, instituted mail-order sales program, and am presently establishing separate bookstore specializing in southwestern art and history as well as allied subjects. Space available will make this largest bookstore dealing in this specialty in the country. Act as paid consultant on sales desks for South-West Regional Museum Conference. Supervise 17 museum employees.

1964–71

OFFICE MANAGER
Sandia Development Corp.
Fieldstone Circle
Albuquerque, New Mexico 87111

Work principally supervisory in this construction company. Directed staff of 44 encompassing bookkeeping, payroll, and drafting departments. Primary responsibility for each department maintaining work schedule. Control and purchase of all office supplies. Directly responsible to vice president of corporation.

1958–64

STORES-KEEPER
Acme Construction Co.
Gladstone Tower
Phoenix, Arizona 85004

Maintained inventory control and issued equipment and materiel. Directly responsible for ordering and allocating materiel requisitioned by engineering department. Supervised 14 office and warehouse workers, some Spanish-speaking.

1955–57	STORES-KEEPER
	Brown, Raymond & Walsh
	Edificio España
	Madrid, Spain

In charge of warehousing, inventory, and issuing all government-supplied material used in U.S. Air Force Base construction. Many of the supplies were critical and required a daily physical count of inventory. Supervised 21 office and warehouse workers, 14 of whom were non-English-speaking Spanish citizens.

Education

1951–55	Middlebury College
	Middlebury, Vermont 05753

B.A. in Spanish Language and Literature. Participated in "Junior Year Abroad" program, attending the University of Madrid in Spain.

References supplied upon request.

FUNCTIONAL RÉSUMÉ

George Roberts 12 Grey Place Albuquerque, New Mexico 87116

Home Phone: (505) 555-1246 Office Phone: (505) 555-2395

Job Objective: A position organizing or developing the sales potential of a museum.

Work History

Museum Sales Director:

Developed energetic sales program, extending existing sales desk, and opening three additional sales points including a young folks' desk and a bookstore specializing in southwestern art, history, and allied subjects. Space available will make this the largest bookstore of its specialty in the country. Also developed mail-order sales program. In five years with the museum, sales have increased by 9600% while traffic through the museum has increased about 300%. Supervise 17 museum employees in sales section. Act as paid consultant on museum sales desks for South-West Regional Museum Conference.

Mission Museum, Albuquerque, New Mexico 87103
  1971–present

Office Manager:

Employment with this construction company was primarily
supervisory. Directed a staff of 44 in bookkeeping, payroll, and
drafting departments. Also purchased and controlled office
supplies. Worked directly under vice president.

Sandia Development Corp., Fieldstone Circle, Albuquerque,
  New Mexico 87111   1964–71

Stores-Keeper:

All functions, including maintaining inventory, ordering and
allocating supplies, supervising assistants in office and
warehouse. Many of assistants did not speak English and had
to be instructed in Spanish.

Acme Construction Co., Gladstone Tower, Phoenix, Arizona
  85004   1958–64

Brown, Raymond & Walsh, Edificio Españo, Madrid, Spain.
  1955–57

Education
———————

B. A., Middlebury College, Middlebury, Vermont 05753
  1951–55

Participated in *Junior Year Abroad* program, attending the
  University of Madrid in Spain.

Personal
————————

Born: February 22, 1933
Height: 6′ 0″
Weight: 165 lbs.
Married, one child
Will relocate

References will be supplied on request.

ANALYTICAL RÉSUMÉ

George Roberts
12 Grey Place   Home Phone: (505) 555-1246
Albuquerque, New Mexico 87116   Office Phone: (505) 555-2395

Job Objective: Application of my proven ability in the field to in-augurating or developing a sales program for a museum.

Qualifications

Museum Sales: As Sales Director for a modest local museum, a small souvenir stand was extended into a full-fledged museum store. In addition a separate young folks' desk was established, and a bookstore, which will soon become the largest in the country specializing in art, history, and allied subjects dealing with the southwestern portion of the United States, has just been inaugurated. In addition, a mail order sales department has been set up. What was an insignificant desk manned by volunteers has become a sales department with 17 paid employees that provides the museum with 32% of its income.

Supervisory Skills: On every job, have been required to supervise and delegate work. At no time have had fewer than 14 assistants in an established job.

Inventory Control: Have full knowledge of inventory procedures, including audit and running inventory. Know requisition, procurement, and supply procedures.

Employers

Mission Museum, Albuquerque, New Mexico 87103, 1971–present

Sandia Development Corp., Fieldstone Circle, Albuquerque, New Mexico 87111, 1964–1971

Acme Construction Co., Gladstone Tower, Phoenix, Arizona 85004, 1958–1964

Brown, Raymond & Walsh, Edificio España, Madrid, Spain, 1955–1957

Education

B.A., Middlebury College, Middlebury, Vermont, 1951–1955

Participated in "Junior Year Abroad" program, attending University of Madrid in Spain.

Personal

Born: February 22, 1933
Height: 6' 0"
Weight: 165 lbs.
          Married, 1 child
          Will relocate

References: On request

SYNOPTIC/AMPLIFIED RÉSUMÉ

Synopsis of Résumé on:

GEORGE ROBERTS
12 Grey Place   Home Phone: (505) 555-1246
Albuquerque, New Mexico 87116   Office Phone: (505) 555-2395

Work Experience

1971–present	SALES DIRECTOR Mission Museum Albuquerque, New Mexico 87103
1964–71	OFFICE MANAGER Sandia Development Corp. Fieldstone Circle Albuquerque, New Mexico 87111
1958–64	STORES-KEEPER Acme Construction Co. Gladstone Tower Phoenix, Arizona 85004
1955–57	STORES-KEEPER Brown, Raymond & Walsh Edificio España Madrid, Spain

Education

1951–55

Middlebury College
Middlebury, Vermont 05753

B.A. in Spanish Language and Literature. Participated in "Junior Year Abroad" program, attending the University of Madrid in Spain.

Personal

Born: 2-22-33   Height: 6′ 0″   Weight: 165 lbs
Married, one child
Will relocate

FOR AMPLIFICATION SEE FOLLOWING PAGE

George Roberts — Amplification of Résumé   Page 2

Work Experience

1971 to present   MISSION MUSEUM

Originally an unpaid volunteer, was offered full charge of sales program of local non-profit private museum. Developed energetic program that resulted, within two years, in sales becoming an important source of museum income. Opened special sales desk for young people, instituted mail-order sales program, and am presently establishing separate museum bookstore specializing in southwestern art and history as well as allied subjects. Space available will make this largest bookstore dealing in this specialty in the country. Act as paid consultant on museum sales desks for South-West Regional Museum Conference. Supervise 17 museum employees.

1964 to 1971   SANDIA DEVELOPMENT CORP.

Work was principally supervisory in this construction company. Directed staff of 44 including bookkeeping, payroll, and drafting departments. Primary responsibility was maintaining work schedules for each department. Also purchased and controlled office supplies. Worked directly under vice president of corporation.

1958 to 1964   ACME CONSTRUCTION CO.

Maintained inventory control and issued equipment and materiel. Directly responsible for ordering and allocating supplies requisitioned by engineering department. Supervised 14 office and warehouse employees, some Spanish-speaking.

1955 to 1957   BROWN, RAYMOND & WALSH

In charge of warehousing, inventory, and issuance of all government-supplied material used in U.S. Air Base construction. Many of supplies were critical and required a daily physical count of inventory. Supervised 21 office and warehouse workers, 14 of whom were non-English-speaking Spanish citizens.

References can be supplied upon request.

CREATIVE RÉSUMÉ

George Roberts

EVEN A NONPROFIT ORGANIZATION RUNS ON MONEY, DOESN'T IT?

After all, contributions are nice, but it's nicer to have a steady source of income to help meet the steady bills.

SOUVENIR STANDS ARE FOR AMUSEMENT PARKS; MUSEUMS NEED SALES DEPARTMENTS.

This is what I can offer you —

My six years of experience with the Mission Museum in Albuquerque, New Mexico.

In that time, a souvenir desk grew to be a full-fledged department, helping the museum meet expenses by contributing 32% of the museum's total budget.

A specialty bookstore has been inaugurated, soon to be the largest of its kind in the country.

A mail-order department furnishes books, art, and museum replicas to buyers across the country.

Expert supervisory ability achieved at the museum and other jobs.

Knowledge of inventory control, a necessity in any retail operation.

In addition to doing a job for the Mission Museum, the South-West Regional Museum Conference has sent me as a paid consultant to 18 different museums in their area to advise on the establishment or development of sales programs.

A B.A. (1955) in Spanish Language and Literature from Middlebury College in Vermont and four years of study and work in Spain have given me a fluency in the language which can be of use in meeting the cultural needs of the burgeoning Hispanic-American community.

For more details, please write me, *George Roberts, 12 Grey Place, Albuquerque, New Mexico 87116*

Putting Yourself on Paper 3

TIP: Your résumé is your personal advertisement.

When writing your résumé, always remember that its purpose is to make you interesting enough to a potential employer to secure you an interview. Your résumé should be considered as an advertisement for yourself and, like a good ad, it should be visually attractive, brief, and informative. Above all, it should create interest in its product. In this case, *you* are the product.

Who Are You? Identify Yourself

Always start with your name, address, and telephone number placed in a conspicuous position. If your résumé is longer than one page, be sure that your name is conspicuously placed on every page.

TIP: Be sure to start with your name.

It is amazing that people would actually go to the trouble of organizing, writing, and having a résumé printed, and then fail to include the essential information that identifies them. I don't know how people can do that, but they do. It happens almost every day.

Of course, my employment agency receives many résumés as part of someone's direct mail campaign, but most are in response to ads we have run in the newspapers. One of our clients, a major law firm, once asked us to recruit an attorney who not only had experience and background in real estate and property taxes, but was also a CPA. We put an ad in the classified columns and received more than forty résumés in reply. Of the forty, only one met the precise requirements. It was well organized and well presented and had only three deficiencies: it lacked a name, an address, and a phone number. You can be sure that this was not the first time, nor will it be the last time, that such an omission kept a job seeker from a job that fitted perfectly.

How Long?

If there is one single cardinal rule in writing a résumé, it is simply this: *Keep it brief!*

TIP: *Be concise and to the point.*

No matter how superior a work history you might have, do your utmost to consolidate it into *one*, or at the very most, *two* pages. Our survey showed that all résumé readers concur in a preference for a concise résumé — not more than two or, in the exceptional case, three pages. These are some of the comments we received:

A personnel manager: "I read about fifty résumés a day and *never* go beyond the second page."

An electronics executive: "I want facts and only the ones I need for a judgment."

A book publisher: "If it's more than three pages, I assume it's an autobiographical manuscript and send it to a junior reader."

A partner in a law firm says: "If the applicant tells me he is expert in probate law, that is all he needs to say on his résumé; I don't need to be told that he knows how to file a will or contest one."

Job Objective or Career Goal

Even though the statement of a job objective is frequently advised in a résumé, a survey done by my employment agency indicates that its inclusion is optional, as most employers are indifferent to its use. If it is stated, it should be placed right after the initial identifying data (name, address, and phone number).

TIP: *The job objective should logically connect with the balance of the résumé.*

The job objective should be brief — one or two lines — and your goal should be justified by the educational and work experience that will follow it.

You should avoid stating an objective that is too confining; you do not want one that will cancel out opportunities you might be interested in. On the other hand, avoid the use of clichés — "A challenging position where I can meet people" — or overly vague generalities — "A job that will interest me and stimulate my best efforts."

Often the job objective can be replaced by a capsule résumé. Not only is the capsule résumé more informative and more interesting to the reader, but it is more likely to have an efficacious result. And that is what you expect from every element of your résumé.

Capsule Résumé

A capsule résumé is a summary in three or four lines of the most pertinent information contained in your résumé. It is the best way of emphasizing a solid work background and of highlighting qualifications appropriate to a specific job opening. While it often involves retyping the résumé, the capsule résumé is a means of directing it to a very concrete offer of employment without having to reorganize the résumé completely.

TIP: A capsule résumé can highlight marketable features of your career.

Consider a hypothetical case. A man has worked fifteen years as a polymer chemist as well as an analytical chemist. His general capsule résumé would read:

> 15 years' experience in the field of organic
> chemistry,

but in answering an ad for a polymer chemist, he would have:

> 15 years' experience in polymer chemistry,
> including a working knowledge of analysis,

and in reply to an ad for an analytical chemist:

> 15 years' concentrated experience in the area of
> analytical chemistry; also work in polymers.

The capsule résumé, if used, should follow your name and address and serve as a headline for the body of your résumé.

The body of your résumé should contain a brief history of your work experience and a concise summary of your education. You can start with either one of the two, but we believe it is best to place the most marketable information first. An experienced person usually starts with the work history, but a newcomer to the job market, with little more than summer or part-time work behind him, would be wiser to begin with an educational summary.

TIP: *If you've had experience, start with your work history, but if you've just graduated from college, start with your educational background.*

ARRANGING YOUR EMPLOYMENT HISTORY

Begin with your present or most recent employment and then work backwards in an inverted chronological order. In this manner, the most important information, which is usually the most recent, is emphasized.

TIP: *Always start with the present or most recent experience and work back into the past.*

Each entry should include the name and address of the employer, the dates involved, the job title, and a brief description of your responsibilities. The description should be succinct and to the point, but should still include all basic activities of each particular job. Use implied pronouns and clear, simple language.

TIP: *Don't write in the third person (he or she). Don't overuse the pronoun "I".*

Writing in the third person is stylistically objectionable. Overuse of "I" is redundant — the person reading the résumé knows you are the subject of your own résumé. For example, don't write:

He supervised a staff of twenty,

or

I supervised a staff of twenty,

but instead:

Superivsed staff of twenty.

Using implied pronouns avoids an impression of boastfulness, on the one hand; and on the other, it gives your résumé a brisk, businesslike air which results in a more professional impression.

Nonetheless, even though you want to strive for brevity in your résumé, avoid the use of abbreviations except in listing your university or professional degrees, such as B.A., Ph.D., C.P.A., or M.S.W. Also be sure that all dates are correct, providing an unbroken sequence, and that there are no spelling or grammatical errors.

EDUCATIONAL HISTORY: COLLEGE OR ADVANCED DEGREE

Your education, like your work history, is arranged in an inverse chronological order. Begin with your most advanced, or most recent, educational experience, and work backwards until you reach your bachelor's degree. If you have already had significant work experience, you simply give the date, the degree, and the name of your school.

TIP: *Always list your most advanced or most significant degree first.*

If you are a college graduate, it stands to reason that you finished high school, so it is not necessary to list it. If your high school or preparatory school is very prestigious, however, naming it may enhance your prospects in certain fields of employment. On the other hand, it may be considered snobbishness on your part and work to your detriment.

TIP: *List all dates.*

Be sure to list all dates of attendance at college as well as date of graduation and the degree received. A recent graduate should include the major and minor study sequences, as well as any academic honors that were earned. If you maintained a high scholastic average (three or four points out of a possible four), you should mention your academic standing. Don't call attention to a mediocre average by mentioning it in your résumé. Of course, any merit scholarships or fellowships should be mentioned.

TIP: *Extracurricular activity can be important.*

If you are a recent graduate, you should list all of your extracurricular activities. Not only does such a list paint a more rounded portrait, but it also indicates talents that are outside of your work experience or areas of study. Membership in your college debating society implies an articulate, poised personality. A class officer will be pictured as an outgoing individual with leadership potential. A staff member of a college publication would usually be seen as appealing in the communications industry.

TIP: *Recent graduates should mention summer or part-time employment.*

Recent graduates should list all of their summer and part-time jobs, even if they have no relationship with present job goals. This experience should, like any other, include names of employers, dates, job titles, and duties. Simply showing that you have worked before is significant to a prospective employer. Experience as a clerk-typist, waiter, babysitter, or anything else will demonstrate an already proven ability and willingness to work. A part-time history establishes the applicant's preparedness to accept responsibility.

EDUCATIONAL HISTORY: NON-COLLEGE GRADUATE

The educational history is handled in the same manner as it is treated by college graduates, if one cannot truthfully claim a college degree.

TIP: *Educational history is important, even if you don't have a college degree.*

The most recent or the present educational experience is placed at the very beginning. If you have attended a trade or business school, or a service-connected or company-sponsored training program, list it with dates of attendance. If high school was the last school you attended, simply list it with appropriate dates.

All certificates, diplomas, and honors should be included. If you supported yourself while studying, be sure to highlight this accomplishment in a prominent manner.

PROFESSIONAL SOCIETIES AND PUBLICATIONS

List all professional associations and organizations that have a bearing on your career goals. Membership in job-related organizations implies dedication to your field of work and an ability to get along with others. For example:

Member, Society of Chemical Engineers; member, Society of Polymer Chemists; Phi Beta Kappa.

List titles of all publications and note when and where they were published. If the list is extensive, merely highlight it and offer a complete list if wanted.

> Published in *Journal of Society of Chemical Engineers* and in *Polymer Chemistry*. List of publications furnished on request.

PERSONAL DATA

Personal data may be included, at your option, in order to provide a more fully rounded picture of you as an individual. This section, by definition, should contain material *pertinent* to the job seeker and his or her qualifications.

However, my agency has actually received résumés that included the job seeker's glove size (the person was *not* looking for a job as a glove model), parents' birthdays, pets' names, and monthly rent and electrical bill. Inclusion of this type of information is not only considered verbose; it's considered in very poor taste.

TIP: *Keep personal data to the minimum — and be honest.*

Information concerning your age, marital status, number of children, height and weight can be included, but this is strictly optional. You might want to include your height and weight in order to give a more three-dimensional picture of yourself. However, if you are overweight — please try to lose weight!

It *is* true that overweight people have more difficulty in finding a job than those who are slim. It's not only a question of appearance; it has to do with the policy of many companies which require a physical examination before making a job offer. Being overweight is considered a health hazard, and many employers are sensitive to this. We once referred to a very well qualified, but 30 pounds overweight, accountant to a Fortune 500 company. He went for the physical exam and was offered the job if he would *promise* to lose weight. He is still on the job — though 25 pounds lighter. However, be particularly careful that if you do carry a few extra pounds and you do mention your weight, *tell it as it is!* When you go for the interview, your slight deviation from the truth will be obvious, embarrassing, and might even cost you the job. Being caught in a lie is usually the kiss of death.

TIP: *Age need not be mentioned.*

Because of recent equal employment acts (especially the Equal Employment Opportunity Act of 1972), it has been illegal for any employer to discriminate because of age, sex or national origin. Employers have been very conscientious about adhering to this. Regarding age, many companies are relearning what they had forgotten as our culture became more youth oriented: that the experience and wisdom that come with maturity are major assets for a prospective employee to offer a company. Therefore, since your age is not allowed to be a factor in your opportunity for employment, it is strictly up to you as to whether or not to include it in your résumé. If you decide to include it, put down your date of birth rather than your current age. Not only is it more professional, but you won't have to update this on your résumé should you later decide to change jobs; you would just have to add information about your current employment. Of course, be completely honest as to your age.

TIP: *Marital status need not be mentioned.*

Marital status is completely optional. Since marital status has absolutely nothing to do with your job qualifications, it really isn't necessary to include such information in your résumé. Keep in mind that according to the Equal Employment Opportunity act, it is against the law to discriminate because of marital status. Remember, we said before that the *only* information *necessary* to include is that which describes your educational and work history.

Many people feel that saying they are married, with children, implies a greater sense of responsibility and hence, more stability. This is not necessarily true. Jobs that require a lot of overtime or travel are often filled more successfully by unmarried people who can be more flexible in terms of time.

Including your marital status is a very personal matter — so whether married, divorced, single, separated, separating, engaged or living with someone, it is strictly your *choice* whether or not you include this confidential information in your résumé. Either decision is acceptable.

HOBBIES AND LEISURE ACTIVITIES

Should you include hobbies and leisure-time activities? You must decide for yourself. If you feel that a description of your avocations will enhance your image, by all means include them.

TIP: *List only those hobbies and activities that can help to describe you.*

A 55-year-old man who participates in outdoor sports should say that he's a sailing enthusiast. This helps the reader of his résumé visualize him as a healthy and active person. After all, despite the jokes about President Ford's falling on the ski slope, most people were aware that a man in his sixties was engaging in a sport that is usually considered an activity for someone thirty years younger.

The hobby of photography would be helpful if you were applying for a reportorial position on a newspaper. Sewing or needlepoint could be of interest on your résumé if you were looking for editorial work on needlework or women's magazines — or any other magazines, as it would show you have the patience for details and ability to concentrate. Even pastimes such as chess or cryptography tend to paint you as a logical and analytical person.

If you include your hobbies on your résumé, there are two things you must remember. First, keep it brief! You don't want to create the impression that all of your time and energy is spent on your hobbies or that you are unable to sustain an interest in one or two avocations and need dozens to fight off boredom. Secondly, be completely honest! Don't put down orchid-growing or gliding because you feel that they are exotic and will make you appear more interesting. They are liable to make you so interesting to the interviewer that things will start off with a discussion of the strange coincidence that the two of you share a common interest in such an esoteric hobby!

MILITARY SERVICE

Completion of military service is of interest to any employer in times of universal conscription. Completion of that service, or a draft-deferred status, should be mentioned on the résumé as a means of assuring the employer that you have an initial intention of being a permanent employee. That is the major reason for including it in a résumé.

Another reason would arise from your military service having a direct effect of your job capabilities. If you had received special technical training in the service and your nonmilitary occupational specialty resulted from that training, both of those facts should be mentioned along with relevant dates and the highest rank achieved.

TIP: Mention your military service so that there is no time lapse in your history.

If your military service has no relevance to your intended work area, it would be best to simply state that you completed military service and were honorably discharged. You could add arm and branch of service if you desire . If you are beyond draft age, there is no point in elaborating on military service unless it adds important occupational information to your résumé.

PERSONAL HISTORY

A short paragraph describing your personal background can be included if you feel that it would offer information not readily discernable from your work or education, but which would add to your marketability. Our survey showed that very few résumé readers feel that it should be included. Most agree that, with only the rarest exceptions, all pertinent information is already included in the résumé.

TIP: *Use personal history only if it makes you more employable.*

Some examples that could be appropriate are :

> Born in Spain of American father and Spanish
> mother. Came to U.S. at age five. Returned to Spain
> with mother every summer. Speak, read, write
> Spanish as fluently as English.

Or take the case of a recent college graduate whose résumé indicated no work experience at all, not even part-time or summer jobs. Her personal history indicated, nonetheless, that she had not been the least bit idle:

> Oldest of four children. Due to mother's death, have
> managed household and supervised younger
> siblings since age fourteen.

Observe that in the first instance, the information offered was valuable to an employer in that it not only claimed fluency in Spanish but corroborated the claim. In the second instance, a responsibility and maturity which belied the lack of work experience was manifested. These are valuable pieces of information; the fact that you were born and raised on Sutton Place or in Bronxville, or that you spent your summers in Bar Harbor and winters in Marbella is not.

LOOK AT ME NOW!

Some people seem to think it is a good idea to include a picture of themselves with the résumé. We have found that most résumé readers react very strongly *against* applicants who enclose photographs.

One personnel director told us, "When I see a photograph, I don't bother reading the résumé. I figure any person counting on looks doesn't have much else to sell."

TIP: *Do not include your photograph.*

A partner in one of the Big Eight accounting firms said, "There are businesses where the employer would like to know what an applicant looks like—some are even legitimate—but ours isn't one of them."

So—while including a photo is not completely taboo, we strongly advise against doing it. It is worth noting that if an offer of employment were to request a résumé *and* a photo, unless it were in the modeling or entertainment fields, it could be considered illegal on grounds that this is a covert form of racial screening. In addition, such a request may indicate that the job has duties other than those normally pertaining to the position offered.

PERSONAL REFERENCES

You should never supply the names of your references in your résumé. Not only is it unprofessional, but it can also cause unnecessary bother to the references listed. You should only give permission to call your references when an employer has indicated that he is really interested in someone with your qualifications.

TIP: Your résumé should NOT contain your references.

Always, of course, get permission from all parties involved to use them as references before releasing their names. Be sure, also, that your references can be reached quickly. For that reason, it is preferable to list people who can be reached by phone rather than by mail. If giving the business phone of a reference, always ascertain that they are still employed by that company.

If your name has changed through marriage or for any other reason during your work or educational history, be sure that your references know you by your new name. It is wise for married women to indicate their maiden as well as married names on the résumé, if the change occurred during any of the résumé history.

REASONS FOR LEAVING PAST JOBS

Your résumé should be a brief summary of your own particular talents, abilities, and qualifications. Since the reasons that you have left previous employment do not add to that summary, they should not be included in your résumé. Like salary requirements, your reasons for having left earlier jobs should be discussed in the interview.

TIP: In your résumé, don't tell why you left previous jobs.

THE BUSINESS OF MONEY

Never discuss salary in your resume — neither minimum salary requirements nor your earnings in the past.

TIP: *Never mention salaries on your résumé.*

Most employers consider salary a most confidential subject. Your résumé will probably be seen by many people in the company who would not be entitled to know your rate of pay, so no indications of it should appear in your résumé. You will have an opportunity to discuss it in the interview. The interviewer should be the one to introduce the subject, and almost certainly will.

TRUTH WILL OUT

Despite our having discussed it earlier, we feel that we cannot overemphasize the necessity of being truthful in all elements of your résumé. It is probable that many lies, half-truths, distortions, or exaggerations will escape detection in an interview. It is even possible that you can get your immediate supervisor in a previous job to back you up. Eventually, however, you will be put to the test and will find that you have not only lost the job, but seriously damaged your prospects for future employment.

TIP: *Remember, honesty is the best policy.*

Often a recently graduated college student, having prepared a résumé, will feel that it is stark and bare and needs "beefing up." Suddenly, it becomes the résumé of a student who completed a bachelor's degree in three years, while holding down a job as a newspaper photographer, editing the college newspaper, working on the staff of the yearbook, holding class office, and graduating with an "A" average. Rather than being astonished by the energy and drive, most résumé readers would shake their heads, and thinking, "This kid has too much biography," throw the résumé into the wastebasket.

Admittedly, there are successful people who bluffed — which is a polite way of saying "lied" — their ways into the positions that started them up the ladder, but you can be assured that there were very few who were able to do so, and many who tried and were found out.

Looking Good!

4

Résumé Appeal

Since your résumé probably will be the first contact between you and your prospective employer, it is imperative that it invite reading. The physical appearance of your résumé is as important as the information it contains. A résumé that is hard to read or confusing to interpret will end up in the wastebasket, while the reader goes on to the next one. Your résumé is competing with many others and as a result is scanned very rapidly. (Our inquiries have shown that personnel offices rarely give more than 30 seconds of attention to a résumé in order to decide if it merits a detailed reading.) The more attractive your résumé is, the better impression it will make in the few moments that are given it initially.

TIP: Be sure your résumé appeals to the eye.

Bearing in mind that your résumé is meant to serve, in part, as a personal advertisement, it would be a good idea to take a hint from the professional ad-makers. As one "pro" expressed it, "A good ad *looks* good enough to grab your attention, and once it's got it, *tells* you what it wants to say as quickly and effectively as it can." Like the ad, your résumé should be visually compelling and brief and to the point.

Cure Your Logorrhea!

Don't run off at the mouth — or, rather, the typewriter. *Keep it brief!* We've already said that, but it can bear repetition because it is important. One page, if possible (and do everything to make it possible); two pages, if necessary; three pages in the rarest and most exceptional cases.

TIP: Remember, keep your résumé brief.

Remember that you are striving for one or two pages. Your résumé should contain just enough information to sketch your abilities and qualifications. It is not an autobiography nor a vehicle for your personal philosophy. Your aim is not to tell the reader all about yourself, but to create enough interest so that the reader will want to know more about you.

Grab the Eye!

The first thing you have to consider before typing the résumé is the layout of the copy. Whether you use one of the samples we will give you or create your own, be sure that the total effect is pleasing to the eye. But be equally sure that it is easy to read and that the different sections are clearly separate from one another.

TIP: *Be sure to have adequate margins.*

Use your ground — the white space on the paper — effectively, even using your margins imaginatively. We have received many résumés whose information indicated easily placed applicants, but that were so badly laid-out and cluttered, that we were hesitant about sending them on to prospective employers. (Note, for example, on our suggested layouts and sample résumés, that there are always at least two spaces between every block of information.)

TIP: *Use standard-size, good-quality paper.*

Even though odd-sized paper might be more arresting visually, it can create a filing problem. Use the standard 8½″ × 11″ paper. It is easily filed and easily handled.

Choose a good quality watermarked bond paper and, if not using white, be sure that is a pale color that will contrast well with the color of the type. Use only one side of the paper, and if the résumé is more than one page, staple the pages together, being sure that your name appears on each page.

TIP: *Proofread your résumé.*

Be sure that there are no spelling or typing errors. It is a good idea to have several people proofread your résumé for you. In addition, unless you are a superlative typist (or plan to have your résumé printed with the printer's own type), it is worth the small expense to have a professional type it for you. If you do so, it would be to your further advantage to find a typist or service which has either a Vari-Typer or an IBM Selectric with different fonts in order to have your résumé laid out with distinctive type faces or section titles.

Reproducing Your Résumé

Once employers expected every résumé they received to be typed individually; fortunately, those days have passed. Although carbon copies (because of smudging and lack of clarity) are not acceptable, any other duplicating process which turns out clean, sharp copies may be used.

TIP: Each copy of your résumé does not have to be individually typed.

Mimeographing, photocopying, offset printing, and multilith processing all give excellent results. Even Xerox copies are acceptable as long as they are sharp and clear. It goes without saying that if you want to spend the money to have your résumé printed from set type, that, too, would be acceptable.

As the success of your job campaign very likely may hinge upon the appearance of your résumé, it is important that you choose a service that turns out a professional-looking product. These services are listed in the Yellow Pages under the heading "Offset Reproductions." Many of them will be able to assist you with the layout and a choice of available type faces.

TIP: When reproducing your résumé, remember to use a good-quality paper.

It is important that your résumé be reproduced on a good quality paper. If you are having a typescript reproduced, it is best to insist upon a good quality watermarked bond. If it is to be printed from cold or hot type, an equally fine opaque paper should be used. Don't be afraid of the additional expense of a quality paper; it will add little to the total cost, and the effect it creates is well worth it.

Model Résumés

On the following pages you will find samples of what we consider to be "job-getting" résumés. Although they represent a variety of fields and a diversification of job categories, you will find they all have several factors in common.

Each résumé is attractively laid out. The important facts and dates are stated simply and clearly. The information contained is consolidated into a reverse chronological history.

If you study the résumés in this section, you will find they all contain the *vital information* as described on page 5. (Note the information that must be included.) Some contain such *optional information* as "job or career objective" while others may include "choices of hobbies or personal histories." Though each of the following résumés contains both marital status and birth date, this is solely for continuity. Remember — this information is optional! (See page 5, and note the items you may or may not include.) Note also that *none* of these résumés includes such information as reasons for leaving past jobs, past, present or expected salaries. (Again, see page 5, and note the section on information never to be included.)

As you browse through these sample résumés, keep in mind what we discussed in Chapter 2 (pages 5 to 17). You will soon get the "feel" of a *better résumé* and will find that writing your own will follow easily.

Index to Model Résumés

The model résumés are organized alphabetically. In some cases there will be several résumés for the same field to show that *every* résumé in a particular field is in itself *unique* and *different*. In other words, each résumé has its singular job descriptions and histories. If you are unable to find a sample résumé fitting your actual job description, model yours after one fitting a similar job title. Note that the résumés have been cross-referenced for your convenience, so you can easily review all résumés under related job titles; those headings with page numbers in italics designate the related job titles.

Though you refer to the following résumés, never copy them or any parts of them. Your own writing will ring truer if it is completely your own work.

Special

Sharon Cook Darrow
65 Elm Street
Kirkwood, Missouri 63122

Telephone: *(314) 653-2244*

Born: May 16, 1941
Height: 5'2"
Weight: 120 lbs.

JOB OBJECTIVE: Accountant

EXPERIENCE:
1965-1979

Howell and Brooks, St. Louis, Missouri
Accountant

Planned and organized own work under some supervision
from the Group Manager. Assisted in determining the
classifications, distribution and recording of
accounting data.

Reconciled discrepancies in subsidiary ledgers and
made proper adjustments. Assisted in the preparation
of standardized accounting reports and statements of
limited scope. Analyzed and interpreted statements
and reports.

1963-1965

Koehler Manufacturing Company, St. Louis, Missouri
Accounting Clerk

Handled basic accounting transactions, coded invoices
for proper distribution, classified transactions and
processed warehouse invoices.

Education

B.S. degree - Community College, St. Louis, Missouri
1962

References

On request.

ACCOUNTANT

Patrick J. O'Marra
45 Hunter Lane
Grand Rapids, Michigan 49505
(616) 432-0146

Date of Birth: 5/6/42
Married / 4 children
5'11'' / 160 lbs.
Will relocate

Job Objective: **Accountant**

Experience

Millbank Furniture Company, Grand Rapids, Michigan

1970-1979

Statistical Specialist – Prepared detailed financial records including status reports, current and historical reports. Prepared journal entries, maintained records for marketing expenditures and inventories. Processed warehouse invoices and prepared sales reports.

1967-1970

Accounts Receivable Analysis Clerk – Made nonstandardized journal entries, coded invoices for proper accounting routing. Analyzed details of regular accounts. Assisted and trained other accounting clerks.

1965-1967

Walker Lumber Company, Inc., Grand Rapids, Michigan

Cash Accounting Clerk – Performed various routine and non-routine bookkeeping and basic accounting tasks including journal entries, verifying data and reconciling discrepancies, preparing detailed reports from raw data, and checking accounting documents for completeness, mathematical accuracy and consistency.

1962-1965

Accounting Clerk Trainee – Operated electronic calculator to make and verify computations. Prepared journal vouchers, entered postings, and filled in standard records and reports. Acquired a working knowledge of such accounting office procedures as posting and balancing, compiling data, preparing summaries, and verifying routine reports by checking against related details and previous data to reconcile irregularities.

Education

Community College — Currently enrolled in a statistics course and completed a two-semester course in mathematics.

Lakewood Business School — Completed courses in basic accounting principles, intermediate accounting, 1963.

Ramsey High School — Graduated with business studies credentials, 1960.

Military

Completed term of service with the National Guard, 1960-1962.

References

On request.

MICHAEL M. DANKO
1233 Ravan Park Avenue
White Plains, New York 10625
(914) 332-2277

JOB OBJECTIVE: Accounting/Finance with management possibilities

EXPERIENCE:

July 1971 to   Mitchell and Kern
  Present   Certified Public Accountants
                  14 Canal Street
                  New York, New York 10003

                  SENIOR ASSISTANT ACCOUNTANT

Employed as a staff accountant to perform basic functions on audit
engagements.

Within two years of employment, promoted to senior assistant accountant
with substantial raise in salary. Work involved increased responsibilities on audits and supervision over staff accountants.

Experienced in various types of commercial audit engagements such as
audits of manufacturing companies, import/export companies, brokerage
engagements, banks and government contractors.

Received exposure in the areas of report drafting, financial statement
preparation and analytic review of operations.

EDUCATION: B.S. Accounting, Columbia University - 1972

PERSONAL: *Born:*   January 10, 1949 - New York City
                  Height: 5'8"
                  Weight: 165 lbs.
                  Health: Excellent

                  References will be forwarded on request.

ACCOUNTING/FINANCIAL ANALYST/ RECENT COLLEGE GRADUATE

GREGORY T. PHILIPS

108-43 Homelawn Street
Jamaica, New York 11432

(212) OL7-8843

Birth Date: *April 7, 1953*
Height/Weight: *5'9", 156 lbs.*
Marital Status: *Single*
Health: *Excellent*

Objective: Challenging position in business management that will allow the opportunity to gain experience in the accounting and finance functions of a large company.

Education: Monroe College, Yonkers, New York
9/75 - present   Currently enrolled in program leading to an M.B.A. Area of concentration is in financial management with special emphasis on the study of accounting for management control.

9/71-5/75   University of Fairfield, Fairfield, Connecticut
B.S. Major in Real Estate and Urban Economic Development. Extensive course work in real property appraisal and investment analysis.

Employment: Monroe College, Yonkers, New York
1/76   Assistant to the manager of analytical studies. (Six-week internship.) Collected and synthesized price data for College's annual inflation study. Project involved library research as well as telephone contact with college suppliers. Internship led to current part-time position of coordinating draft for final report.

6/74   Eaton Real Estate, New Canaan, Connecticut
Real estate salesperson. Employed part-time by Eaton for the purpose of buying and selling real property.

9/73-6/75   University of Fairfield, Fairfield, Connecticut
Head resident. Responsible for running all aspects of a college dormitory. Duties included supervising residents, kitchen and maintenance staff and preparing all paperwork for Department of Student Affairs. Job was concurrent with full-time academic study to earn seventy percent of college expenses.

Summers: Monroe College, Yonkers, New York
Dispatcher: Employed by physical plant department with responsibility for keeping accurate records on thirty-vehicle motor pool.

Groundsperson: Responsible for maintenance of college buildings and grounds.

References: Available upon request.

ACCOUNTING TRAINEE

Edward T. Washington
48-01 129th Street
New York, New York 10021
(212) 794-2376

OBJECTIVE:	Junior Accountant/Auditor Trainee
EDUCATION:	Hunter College, B.B.A. 1976 - Major: Public Accounting York Community College, A.A. 1974 - Major: Business Administration
GENERAL BACKGROUND:	Five years' professional experience utilizing customer relations and general accounting principles with the following firms:

Adjustments	Banker's Trust Co., New York, N.Y. 1973-Present
Accounts	Western Union Co., New York, N.Y. 1971-1973

SPECIFIC EXPERIENCE:	Adjustments	Inscribing amounts on checks from different branches of banking established throughout United States; balancing customer accounts by keeping accurate records of payments and adjustments; exacting time-keeping records and forwarding to payroll division.
	Accounts	Processing and recording Western Union accounts including heavy customer contacts; keeping daily records of accounts receivable; acting as liaison between customer and accounting division; disseminating general information into specific codes for business purposes involving written correspondence and interpretative designs.

COLLATERAL
COURSES:

Law, Management Science, Computer Information Science, Marketing, Business Management, Calculus, Statistics, Financial Analysis, Individual Taxation, Partnership Corporation Taxes, Estates and Trusts, Electronic Data Processing, and Advanced Professional Auditing (one year). Advanced Accounting practice. Seminar in Accounting, Specialized Accounting.

(Continued)

AFFILIATION: | <u>Voluntary Emergency Corp</u>.- Helping in emergency services.
<u>Hunter College Accountants' Society</u>.

INTERESTS: | Photography and Sports.

PERSONAL DATA: | Age 24 - Geographical preference - New York Metropolitan Area
Single - 5'10" - 175 lbs.

REFERENCES: | Available upon request.

ELLEN A. BRZOWSKI
81 St. Marks Place
New York, New York 10037

(212) 559-9630

———————————————————

VICTOR TEMPORARIES (1972 - To Date)
  New York, New York

Assistant to President
Interview applicants
Liaison with clients
Telephone sales
Bookkeeping

AMERICAN MOTORS CORPORATION (1969 - 1972)
  White Plains Zone Office

Assistant Office Manager (Government Bonded)
Responsible for:
Expense accounts for - sales representatives,
district managers and all zone office personnel.
Travelletter authorizations.
Accident reports.
Accounts payable and receivable.
Zone sundry reports for car distribution.
'Parts' account for twenty-eight General Motors
dealers.

REVLON (1965-1968)
  New York Office

Supervisor of Order Department
Responsible for:
Liaison with cosmetic buyers of superior store chains.
Supervised eight members of staff.
Organized promotional material for new items.
In charge of setting up new accounts.

MARTIN CARPETS (1963-1965)
  Brookfield, Connecticut

Assistant Manager
Customer relations
Sales representative
New accounts establishment   (Continued)

(Personal)

Yorktown Teachers College (1961 - 1963)
A.S. Business Administration

DATE OF BIRTH: 1-5-43   MARITAL STATUS: Single
HEIGHT/WEIGHT: 5'5"/125

_____

References will be furnished on request.

DEAN ASHER

Address   49 W. Mangnot Lane
Easton, Vt. 05341

Telephone   Home: 919–619–0936
Service: 800–616–0319

Vital Statistics   Age: 26   Height: 6'2"   Weight: 160 lbs.   Born: November 12, 1949

Work Experience   1974–1979: Researcher/Technical Editor, Lipcot-Abbey-McLoyton-Thomas-McCarthy-Stratton (Engineers and Architects), 345 Park Avenue, New York, Department of Environmental Planning and Socioeconomic Studies. Assembled information concerning complicated and sensitive subject matter through personal contacts; researched documents, statutes and governmental procedures; set style and format; edited and proofread environmental impact statements and proposals.

1974: Assistant to the publicity director, Mainman Ltd., 405 Park Avenue, New York. Assisted with ad campaigns, preparation of press kits, news releases, publicity events and planning of Times Square spectacular billboard for RCA recording artists.

1973: Reporter/Ad Salesman, The Lower Cape, Provincetown, Massachusetts. Covered local news stories for shoppers' guide and local news weekly publication.

1972: Customer Service, U.S. Committee for UNICEF, 331 Easton Street, Easton, Vermont. Responsible for personal correspondence concerning customer complaints and orders in the greeting card program.

1968–1972: Journalist, U.S. Navy. Aboard an LST in Vietnam, inaugurated a campaign of hometown news releases and stories of shipboard life with the riverine forces in the Mekong Delta. Public Affairs Office, Third Naval District Headquarters, San Jose. Wrote news releases, photographed and organized mass media command presentations, press contact at official ceremonies and admiral's aide at social engagements.

Education

Department of Defense Information School (DINFOS) Fort Harrison, Indiana	Graduate, 1970 Journalism/Public Relations
Northwestern University National High School Institute Evanston, Illinois	Graduate, 1966 Speech/Drama
Mid Prairie Community High School Wellman, Iowa	Graduate, 1962

(Continued)

Honors   Alternate Delegate to the World Youth Assembly, 1970.
United Nations, New York City

Organizations   Executive Secretary for the Neighbors of Teilson Park, YMCA.

Interests   International Politics, Current Affairs, Parapsychology, Yoga.

Recommendations furnished upon request.

ADMINISTRATIVE ASSISTANT

Rose J. Martinson
43 Racine Avenue
Skokie, Illinois 60076

(312) 546-7898

Born: September 21, 1941
Status: Single
Height: 5'5"
Weight: 112 lbs.

Job Objective:
Administrative Assistant

Experience
1970-1979

Howard T. Mack, Inc.   Skokie, Illinois

Assistant to the president and owner of this firm dealing in
rare coins and stamps. The president, who travels extensively,
is primarily concerned with purchasing large collections and
negotiating financial transactions involving the expansion of
company operations through new investments.

Responsible for employment, training, salary administration,
and terminations for 150 employees. Supervisor of four departments: bookkeeping, shipping, direct mail sales, and customer
relations. Determine adjustments and credits on customer
transactions. Responsible for the monthly distribution of
want lists to over 300 dealers. Determine bid and purchase
price on coins and stamps from private collections.

1966-1970

The Field Foundation   Chicago, Illinois

Assistant to Director of Office Services. Supervised office
staff of thirty clerical, stenographic, and machine operator
personnel. Interviewed applicants, trained new employees,
scheduled work assignments, and made equipment changes to
improve efficiency.

1963-1966

Northwestern University   Chicago, Illinois

Assistant to Placement Director. Job searched and placed
undergraduate students in part-time jobs. Met with recruitment representatives from industry and arranged interviews
for them with students who were completing graduate work.
For the first two years in this capacity, performed routine
clerical and secretarial tasks.

Education

Northwestern University - A.B. degree, June 1963

History Major and Psychology Minor. Junior Class President.

References

On request.

ADMINISTRATIVE SECRETARY

ALVARO SUAREZ
40 West 72nd St.
New York, N.Y. 10023
212-787-0871

PERSONAL DATA

Born: November 18, 1944
Marital Status: Married, no children
Height: 5'8", Weight 145 lbs.

EXPERIENCE

1974–
1979
Personal Secretary to First Secretary of Dominican Republic to the United Nations, New York. Handled all personal correspondence, prepared all details for major international sports events in Dominican Rep., arranged housing and entertainment for dignitaries visiting Mission to the U.N. Acted as interpreter.

1971–
1974
Administrative Assistant and Secretary, ANCO International, New Jersey. Served in this capacity to President of this corporation. Assumed responsibility for office in his absence, including handling of all correspondence, translations in Spanish and Italian, transcribing of large volume of shorthand as well as dictaphone-typing; made arrangements for hotel accommodations and booked space for conferences, both domestic and overseas. Acted as interpreter for foreign company representatives visiting New York.

1970–
1971
Executive Secretary to the Director of International Operations, Standard Tobacco International, New York. Handled all press contacts, translated foreign press releases, assumed all secretarial responsibilities, and assisted in all public relations activities.

1965–
1970
Executive Secretary/Assistant Fashion Coordinator, Longine-Pioneer Corporation, New York. Translated fashion copy for magazines and newspapers, prepared press parties, fashion shows, performed secretarial duties.

EDUCATION
B.A. in Social Studies, 1965 – University of Santo Domingo, Dominican Republic

LANGUAGES
Fluency in Spanish, Italian, English

SECRETARIAL SKILLS
Typing: 85 wpm; Steno: 90 wpm. Dictaphone

PERSONAL INTERESTS
Art exhibits, travel, symphonic music, poetry

REFERENCES
On request.

ADVERTISING EXECUTIVE

NAME: David R. Chosack

ADDRESS: 987 Chicago Street
            St. Louis, Missouri   63101
            (314) 548-4375

EXPERIENCE:

Kenyon and Eckhardt, Inc. April 1969-June 1978. Hired as Account
Coordinator for Air France, Helena Rubinstein, and Foreign Vintage
accounts. In addition to the regular duties, other responsibilities
as coordinator were to check the monthly production invoices prior to
their submission to the client and to insure that an ad was released
to a publication for every insertion placed on a media estimate. The
Anaconda, French West Indies Tourist Board, Royal Air Maroc, and Alfred
Dunner accounts were added to the coordinating assignments.

In March 1972, promoted to Account Executive on Air France account.
During past three years gained experience in supervising all facets
of the account. In detail, this included initiating and approving
overall campaigns, writing copy, planning media and complete supervision of print, radio, and TV production.

Doyle Dane Bernbach, Inc. June 1966-April 1969. Hired specifically
to traffic portions of the Monsanto account in TV and print. Handled
these portions until February 1967, then was transferred to the tire
and corporate divisions of Uniroyal (TV and print). During this time,
also assisted with traffic on Sony, portions of Burlington Industries
and other house accounts. Subsequently, the shoe and golf ball divisions of Uniroyal and American Tourister Luggage were added.

McCall Corporation. December 1962-June 1966. Position as Assistant
Advertising Quality and Control Manager for production department
of McCall's Magazine. Channeled flow of plates from various advertising agencies throughout the United States to our printing plant
in time for each closing date of McCall's and Redbook magazines. Had
gained experience in control of color quality as well as in the
ordering of safety shells and electros.

In January 1966, promoted to the position of Advertising Traffic
Manager. In this capacity had complete charge over the responsibilities listed above, in addition to supervising a small staff.

(Continued)

Kaiser, Sedlow & Temple. December 1961-December 1962. Started with Burke, Charles and Guignon Advertising as Traffic Manager. When agency merged with Kaiser, Sedlow & Temple in June 1962, continued as Traffic Manager and Media Director on Twentieth Century Fox, Columbia Pictures, Embassy Pictures, and Arco Lighting.

Compton Advertising Agency. August 1960-October 1961. Started as messenger in traffic department and gradually assisted Traffic man with accounts such as Kelly-Springfield and some Proctor and Gamble Company products.

AGE:	March 26, 1939 -- date of birth
MARITAL STATUS:	Married, 2 children
ARMED FORCES:	U.S. Army -- August 1957-August 1960
EDUCATION:	Queens and City Colleges

ADVERTISING/MARKETING COORDINATOR

Gregory L. Charleston
78 Oaktree Drive
Philadelphia, Pennsylvania 19012
(215) 547-9834

PERSONAL

Born 7-24-37; Married.
Six years U.S. Air Force. Made rank of Captain.

PROFESSIONAL
EXPERIENCE

LENOX CHINA/CRYSTAL   Trenton, N.J. 8-74 to present
Coordinator of Advertising and Promotion

* Hold responsibility for production and printing of all
  4-color sales promotional materials, including catalogs.
* Write original copy, supervise others in copy writing,
  artwork, layouts and production.
* Supervise production of dealer newspaper portfolio.
* Work on designs for p.o.p. materials and displays.
* P.R. release preparation and agency coordination.
* Supervise copy, preparation, and production of retail
  store envelope enclosure program.
* Budget work, have submitted several substantial cost
  reduction items.
* Trade show supervision and participation.
* Arrange and coordinate national press show.
* Sales meeting preparation and assistance.

BUSINESS NEWS, INC.   Philadelphia, Pa.   1-73 to 7-74
Associate Advertising Sales Manager

* Account supervisor, sold and serviced over 500 accounts.
* Supervised in-house agency services for clients, including
  copy, ad design, production and media planning.
* Wrote P.R. releases for clients.
* Did publication expansion research.
* Increased commission rate from $10 K/yr. to $17 K/yr. in
  eighteen-month period.

DUN & BRADSTREET, INC.   Philadelphia, Pa.   8-72 to 1-73
Credit Services Salesman

MASSACHUSETTS MUTUAL LIFE INSURANCE COMPANY, 1-70 to 7-72
Life and Health Sales -- Honolulu, Hawaii, Allentown, Pa.

(Continued)

EDUCATION   Muhlenberg College, Allentown, Pa., B.A. in Psychology
                   U.S. Air Force Telecommunications-Electronics Management
                   School
                   Charles Morris Price School of Advertising
                   Sales and Marketing Schools

OBJECTIVE   Growth-oriented position in advertising-marketing.
                   References provided by request.

AIRLINE RESERVATIONIST

Maria Zawacki
68 Old Mill Road
Springfield, Michigan   48678
(313) 821-9641

Job Objective: To function as airline reservationist or reservations supervisor.

Experience

4-69-present   Reservationist, Great North Airlines, Detroit, Mich. Make reservations for GN Airlines to all locations in United States and Canada; arrange connecting flights, teletype and receive information.

7/60-4/69   Reservationist, Trans-West Airlines, Chicago, Ill. Performed all reservation duties at O'Hare Airport; arranged connecting flights; type and teletype; operated small computer.

Education

June 1960   Graduated from Laverne Bell Modeling School, Chicago, Ill.

June 1959   Commercial Diploma
Mother Seton High School, Chicago, Ill.

Hobbies   Cooking, Travel, Photography, Swimming

Personal   Date of Birth: September 8, 1941
Height: 5'8"
Weight: 130 lbs.
Marital Status: Widowed, one child

References   Full references will be furnished on request.

**Resume of
WILLIAM A. ELLIOTT**

20 Jerome Drive
Putnam Lake
Patterson, N.Y. 12563

EDUCATION

1955-1958, P.S. 89, Brooklyn, New York. 1958-1962, Erasmus Hall High School, Brooklyn, New York. 1962-1965, School of Visual Arts, 209 E. 23rd Street, New York, New York. Graduated with Associates Degree.

EMPLOYMENT

10/69 to present — For the past five years worked for the New York Zoological Society as a Designer-Illustrator. During the last two years held a supervisory position as the assistant Art Director. Duties included designing of all printed material used for the Zoo and Aquarium. (Annual reports, educational brochures, books, posters, letterheads, logos.) Was also involved in the design and production of all the educational graphics that appear both outside and inside the buildings. All of the above mentioned work was designed and produced on the Zoo's property.

Additional Experience — Three years' experience operating a 20x24 Chemco copy camera. Five years experience silk screening multicolor back-lit graphics.

1/69 - 10/69 — R. H. Macy's — Advertising. Worked free lance for Macy's designing all advertising for 22 departments such as Cosmetics, Jewelry, Children's Apparel, Sporting Goods, etc.

1966 - 1968 — U. S. Army. Worked as Post Illustrator at Ft. Richardson, Alaska, during which time designed displays for A.U.S.A. Convention held in Washington, D.C. in September, 1966. Also worked on the designing and construction of displays used in the commemoration of the Alaskan Centennial. Transferred to White Sands Missile Range, New Mexico, where worked on several Army promotional displays.

PERSONAL

Born 5/6/45 in New York City. Height 6'1'', Weight 190. Married, 2 children. Health, good. Hobbies, fly fishing, and fly tying. Affiliations: Society of Animal Artists, Southern New York Fish & Game Association, Trout Unlimited.

Bill Elliott wildlife illustrator
animal portraits wildlife illustration birds·fish·mammals 914-279-9338

ART DIRECTOR

CONSTANCE ANITA KRAVITZ
456 Philadelphia Road
Camden, New Jersey 08705

Unmarried
5'3" - 112 lbs.
Born: May 29, 1947

BUSINESS EXPERIENCE

Electronics Age Magazine
CHILTON PUBLISHING COMPANY

1971 to present

Assistant Art Director - March 1973 to present
Report to Art Director and Managing Editor.
Responsibilities include art selection and preparation, illustrating, magazine layout, and some cover
design. When necessary, act as a Chilton representative at our printer's and serve in a supervisory
capacity. Position involves heavy contact with
artists, writers, editors, and suppliers and the
ability to work under tight deadlines.

Production Editor - November 1971 to March 1973
Responsible for all copy flow on Electronics Age.
Programmed software on Typeset 8 system for computer
typesetting. Served as liaison between art and
editorial departments and between the printer, various
vendors and the magazine. Completed a work flow
analysis/time-motion study to determine more efficient
production processes which recently resulted in a re-
allocation of personnel.

GREYSTONE PUBLISHING (Franson Corporation)

June 1971 to
November 1971

Production - Position included responsibility for the
design and layout of decorating encyclopedias. Was
working art director for a short time before leaving.
Much work done in the area of paste-up and mechanicals,
line drawings, type spacing and other duties involving
direct mail pieces.

DAN RIVER MILLS

January 1971
to June 1971

Commercial Artist - Originated fabric design on hand
loom.

(Continued)

THE TEXAS CATHOLIC NEWSPAPER   Dallas, Texas

January 1969   <u>Staff Artist</u> - Job entailed complete responsibility for
to January 1971 all art work associated with the paper itself and its
                 advertising. Also estimated the amount of advertising
                 and editorial copy per issue and determined the forms
                 accordingly. Designed cover and produced the Diocesan
                 Directory for 1971.

September 1971   HUNTER COLLEGE   C.C.N.Y.
to present   Studio and Art History Major/English minor

September 1965   UNIVERSITY OF DALLAS   Irving, Texas
to June 1967   Fine Arts Major

ART DIRECTOR

MORRIS LEVINE
21 East 50th Street
New York, New York 10017
(212) 966-0561

PERSONAL

Date of Birth - February 11, 1940
Married, 4 children
6'2", 200 lbs.

OBJECTIVE: Growth position that would
effectively utilize my experience as commercial artist.

EXPERIENCE

1971-present   Art Director, Schirmer Graphics Company. Create original
art for audio-visual shows and slide production, mechanicals
for annual report production, and photography.

1966-71   Assistant Art Director, Grosset Publications, Inc.
Circulation Art Department. Created direct mail pieces,
sales aids promotions, product ads, rate cards, logos and
letterheads, 4-color brochures, spot drawings and slides,
from concept to completion.

1961-66   Assistant Art Director, Creative Arts Magazine Enterprises.
Created sales aids promotions, direct mail pieces, product
ads, research studies, rate cards, brochures, logos and
letterheads, inserts, rough and semi-comps.

1959-61   Assistant Art Director, Mechanical Designs Magazine.
Emphasis on general boardwork, layout, mechanicals, photo
cropping and scaling, spot drawings.

1957-59   Staff Artist, Clint Crafts Publishers, Art Department.
General boardwork, layout, mechanicals, photo cropping
and scaling.

EDUCATION

Industrial Arts High School - Graduated June, 1957, Commercial Arts Diploma.

INTERESTS

Textile painting, needlepoint design, horseback riding, tennis.

REFERENCES

Furnished upon request.

RESUME OF
LAURIE ADAMS

ADDRESS   24 Oak Park Road
Peekskill, New York 11304
(914) 341-4416

PERSONAL   Born: May 25, 1953
Marital Status: Single
Height: 5'5"
Weight: 125

EDUCATION   1971-1975: Brown University, B.A. Studio Art.
Includes study at Sir John Cass School of Art, London, England,
and Rhode Island School of Design.

1968-1971; Morristown High School, Morristown, N.J.

1970: Syracuse University, Photography and Art Workshop.

EMPLOYMENT   1975-Present: General boardwork, Design Plus Inc., Yorktown Heights, N.Y.

1975-Summer: General boardwork, High Times Magazine, New York, N.Y.

1972-Summer: Mechanical, paste-up artist,
Lasky Company Lithographers, Millburn, N.J.

1970-Summer: Art Instructor, Camp Rondack, N.Y.

**HONORS AND
AWARDS**   Salutatorian, Morristown High School.
First Prize, Art Contest, City Federal Bank.
Alumni Award, Morristown High School.
National Merit Scholarship Semi-Finalist.

ACTIVITIES   College: Art Students' Group, counseling program.
Hobbies: Swimming, tennis, guitar.
Languages: Good command of French. Read Spanish.

REFERENCES   Available on request.

ATTORNEY

John Corwin
62 Pine Street
Scarsdale, New York 10583
(914) 823-1234

EXPERIENCE:

1/71 - Present   ASSOCIATE COUNCIL
                      Sklar Paints, Inc.
                      Yonkers, New York

                      RESPONSIBILITIES:
                      Trade regulation/restrictive business practices
                      counseling. Monitor compliance with *FTC* Consent
                      Decrees.
                      Draft and review *contracts*, including: distributor-
                      ships; licenses (patent, know-how, trademark);
                      import/export; purchase and sale of goods, services,
                      businesses; joint ventures; leases, realty, secrecy,
                      employment; secured transactions.
                      Negotiate warranty and product liability claims.
                      Review with management foreign legal require-
                      ments, and implement appropriate action.
                      Coordinate litigation in conjunction with local
                      trial counsel.
                      Maintain corporate records for various subsidiaries.

EDUCATION: New York University
                     Graduate School of Law
                     LL.M., January 1971
                     Class standing - Top Quarter

                     New York Law School
                     J.D. January 1970
                     Class standing - Top Quarter

                     Cornell University
                     B.A. June 1967
                     Class standing - Top Quarter

PERSONAL: Birthdate: 6/5/45
                     Height: 5'10"
                     Weight: 165 lbs.
                     Marital Status: Married

References available upon request.

Teresa Ortega
1852 Palm Springs Blvd.
Miami, Florida 33182
(305) 890-8342

Career Objective

To utilize my biochemical expertise
in the area of medical research.

Experience

Biochemist, South Florida Medical Center, 9/68-7/78.
Supervised staff of sixteen chemists, biologists and
lab technicians. Set up procedures for analysis of
organic and inorganic compounds for both quality and
quantity. Was responsible for scheduling and planning experiments, maintaining all records in laboratory manual; in charge of test animals, dissections,
blood, tissue tests.

Education

M.S. Biology, Columbia University,
1968

B.S. Chemistry, Smith College, 1966

Personal

Date of Birth: 6/16/45   Hobbies: Chess
Height: 5'2"   Sailing
Weight: 105 lbs.   Reading
Marital Status: Single

References on request

BOOKKEEPER

Pablo Gonzalez
12 Prickly Pear Road
Santa Fe, New Mexico 87524
(505) 239-8765

POSITION OBJECTIVES

Desire to be Manager or Assistant Manager of a
dynamic Accounting Department or Division with
opportunities to be Assistant Controller.

WORK HISTORY

1973 - present
Supervisor - Accounts Payable, White's, Santa Fe.
Supervise 5 people; process approx. 15 to 40
vendor adjustments and inquiries per day; handle
accruals and reconciliations both quarterly and
yearly.

1970-1973
Manager - Accounts Payable, Quality Foods, Santa Fe.
Supervised 25 people; processed approximately 600
invoices per day; audited vendor invoices for payment;
handled vendor adjustments and inquiries.

1960-1970
Assistant Manager - Accounts Payable, Pop-Rite Soda,
Los Angeles. Supervised 17 people; processed approximately 500 invoices per day; balanced daily disbursements with computer printout.

1955-1960
Billing Supervisor, Gardner Advertising, Los Angeles.
Supervised 5 people; billed approximately 40 invoices
per day; Accounts Receivable and Accounts Payable.

Personal

Height - 5'10"
Weight - 185 lbs.
Date of Birth - 11/2/34
Marital Status: Married,
 4 children

Education

Santa Fe High, Commercial Course

Military Service

U.S. Navy, 1952-1955,
Honorable Discharge.

REFERENCES SUPPLIED BY REQUEST.

BOOKSTORE MANAGER/SELLER

MILLARD POLLOCK
1428 Cornelia
Brooklyn, N.Y. 11227
(212) EV 4-3366

Date of Birth: May 30, 1952
Height and Weight: 6'3", 226 lbs.
Marital Status: Married

OBJECTIVE: To manage a general bookstore with large volume sales, and
act as buyer for same. Particularly interested in rare
editions and current literature.

EXPERIENCE

May 1974-
Present

Store Manager, R. Altman Bookseller, Riverdale, New York.
Responsible for increase in sales of at least 25% since
handling of inventory and selection of items for special
sales. Present sales volume more than 20% above previous
goal.

February 1973-
May 1974

Manager Trainee, R. Altman Bookseller, Daytona Beach,
Florida. Trained in all phases of selling, customer
relations, sales presentations, etc.

May 1972-
February 1973

Sales Clerk, Bainbridge Music Sales, Inc., Springfield, Ohio.
Sold sheet music; recommended special pieces for chorale
groups, instrumentalists.

EDUCATION

Attended University of Kansas September 1970 through June 1972.
Majored in Literature.

P.S. 68, Brooklyn - 1966-1969 - College Prep. Curriculum.

PROFESSIONAL AFFILIATIONS

Member of NBS. Certified completion of NBS/FLS Booksellers Program.

INTERESTS

Collecting lithographs, antique watches and first edition volumes;
reading.

REFERENCES

Complete references will be furnished upon request.

Laura Sue Carter
236 West Street
Hendersville, N.C. 27208

Home: (919) 421-1234
Work: (919) 472-9200

PROFESSIONAL
   OBJECTIVE   Sports Wear Buyer

BUSINESS EXPERIENCE

   1972 to present   **Sports Wear Buyer**, Playtime, Inc., Waring, N.C.
                            Complete charge of women's sportswear department, responsible
                            for $300,000 budget; supervise staff of 6 junior buyers; check,
                            authorize payment on all invoices.

   1967 to 1972   **Assistant Buyer**, Kronfeld's, Hendersville, N.C.
                            Responsible for checking and verifying the merchandise; coded
                            tags and records; handled all secretarial duties.

   EDUCATION   B.A. 1967, Wake Forest, Fine Arts

   PERSONAL   Date of Birth: 3/21/45
                            Married   5'6"   125 lbs.
                            No Children

David Hershfield
166 Elm Street
Framingham, Mass. 02189
(617) 421-6822

Objective   To secure a position for the summer of 1976
                 as an athletic or senior counselor. Full Red
                 Cross training and qualifications.

Experience   Athletic Counselor, Camp Wee-ta-kee, Geneva, N.Y.,
                 summer of 1975. Responsible for all sports for
                 the 14- to 16-year-old age group; sports included
                 swimming, tennis, archery and riding; supervised
                 junior counselors.

                 Waterfront Counselor, Camp Endicott, Turham, N.H.,
                 summer of 1974. Supervised all lake sports,
                 including canoeing, sailing, swimming, and water
                 skiing.

                 Counselor, Camp Endicott, summer of 1973.
                 Responsible for 65 boys; instructor in basketball.

Education   Junior at University of Pennsylvania.

Personal   Born March 12, 1956; Height 6'2"; weight 190 lbs.;
                 Single.

References   References on request.

CASHIER

ROBERTA CALDWELL
35 Lyndon Way
Cromwell, New Jersey 07841

201-991-0328

Born June 8, 1927
5'7½", 145 lbs.
Married, 2 teenage sons

OBJECTIVE: To be employed as cashier in large retail store
              in shopping center, preferably in Cromwell vicinity.

EXPERIENCE

1966-   **Cashier**, part-time, Bergen Supermarket, Bergen, N.J.
1979   Worked 20 hours a week as cashier at checkout counter.

1948-   **Assistant Bookkeeper and Cashier**, Howard's Retail Store.
1951   Collected and recorded mail-order payments as well as
          those made in person at credit office; prepared monthly
          statement; assisted bookkeeper in all record-keeping.

1946-   **Accounts Receivable Clerk**, Homowak Mart, New Bergen, N.J.
1948   Received payments made in credit office and by mail,
          recorded cash, issued receipts. Prepared monthly state-
          ments to customers.

EDUCATION

1945   Completed six months' course in Business Machines at
          Cromwell Business School.

1941-   Attended Cromwell High School. Completed requirements
1945   for Commercial Diploma.

INTERESTS

Gourmet cooking, sewing, pen-and-ink drawing.

REFERENCES

Furnished upon request.

CIRCULATION MANAGER

Robert S. Showalter
135 Maine Avenue
Flushing, New York 11353
(212) 533-6857

Married, Two Children
Date of Birth: June 2, 1925

SUMMARY:

Circulation management executive. Consumer, trade, business publishing
fields. Total expertise in all circulation areas, including subscription
promotion, direct response, graphics buying, agency sales, newsstand
sales, fulfillment, computerized systems, budgets, audit requirements.

EMPLOYMENT:

Mailis Publishing Co., Inc., New York, New York. (9/74 - present)
Circulation director and member of management planning board.
Responsible for the development and implementation of all circulation
and related programs. Initiated and implemented merchandise marketing
program.

Reader's Digest, Inc., Mount Kisco, New York. (1/74 - 8/74)
Assistant to vice president and circulation director. Involvement
included all circulation areas, subscription promotion, direct response
programs, agency sales, fulfillment, budgets.

Food Packaging, Inc., New York, New York. (2/72 - 12/73)
Assistant to vice president and circulation director. Responsibilities
included all circulation areas, subscription promotion, direct response
programs, agency sales, newsstand, fulfillment, budget.

Computer/Data, Inc., New York, New York. (2/49 - 6/72)
Operations manager for computerized magazine, book, direct mail,
merchandise fulfillment and related services.

EDUCATION:

Francis Lewis High School, Queens Village, New York
Queens College, Flushing, New York (1946 - 1949)
Hunter College's School of Advanced Business Administration (1950 - 1951)

MILITARY:

U.S. Army (1943 - 1945)

Active duty: Non-commissioned officer in charge of group operations.
Honorable discharge with rank of M/Sgt.

REFERENCES:

Available on request.

CLERK

Raymond J. Stetson

99 Perry Street
New York, New York 10014

212-924-8813 (home)
212-879-5500 (business)

Date of Birth: December 10, 1947

Social Security: 147-38-8482

Marital Status: Single

Professional Experience:

7/73-Present
Clerk, The Metropolitan Museum of Art, 5th Avenue and 82 Street, New York, New York 10028. Knowledge of all aspects in production and composition of internal museum publications. Responsibilities include photography, reduction, layout, sizing and printing.

1/72-7/73
Clerk and Assistant Bookkeeper, Basic Books Co., 208 W. 53 Street, New York, New York 10022. Dealings in royalty allotments to educational publications' authors, including company as well as author dividends. Also development of a computerization layout and feed-in to replace manual computations.

12/70-1/72
Intermediate Clerk, First Jersey National Bank, 1 Exchange Place, Jersey City, New Jersey 07302. Solely responsible for computer feed-in of dealer commissions for mutual funds corporations. Control check of stock books and balancing.

7/65-11/66
Clerk, First Jersey National Bank, 1 Exchange Place, Jersey City, New Jersey 07302. Accounts researcher, stock issuance, control of accounts receivable for mutual funds corporations. Daily use of telephone for communication of services to nationwide investors and their representatives.

Military Experience:

12/66-11/70
Aviation Electronics Technician, United States Navy. Honorable Discharge. Training in internal circuit operations of aviation electronic components and computers.

(Continued)

Educational Background:

     B.A., City College of New York, New York, New York. 9/73-6/76.
     Area of major concentration, Art History.

     Montclair State College, Upper Montclair, New Jersey. 9/71-6/73.
     Area of major concentration, English.

     St. Peters College, Jersey City, New Jersey. 9/65-6/66.
     Area of major concentration, Mathematics.

References:

     Available upon request.

CLERK-TYPIST

EVELYN PLUMER
259 Ridge Lane
Danbury, Connecticut   06810
203-742-3301

PERSONAL

Birth Date: July 23, 1951
5'6", 124 lbs.
Single

> JOB OBJECTIVE: To provide top-quality, con-
> scientious service as typist and office clerk
> to industrial firm in New York City.

EXPERIENCE

1971-
Date
: **Typist, File Clerk**, Feinberg Associates, Danbury, Connecticut. Assemble data from legal reports, type revisions and legal contracts; serve as relief receptionist, maintain files and provide general office assistance.

1968-
1971
: **Typist-Receptionist**, Manzo Realtors, Forest Hills, New York. Served as receptionist to large Real Estate company; typed documents related to sale and purchase of property; filed records of clients and construction companies; maintained appointment schedules.

EDUCATION

Graduated with Commercial Diploma from Danbury High School, June, 1968.

OFFICE SKILLS

Typing - 75 wpm; Shorthand - 100 wpm; Filing; Calculators; Dictaphone; Duplicating Machines; Call Directors.

HOBBIES

Water Skiing, Miniature Golf, Table Tennis

REFERENCES

Will be provided upon request

Chiala Dakazarom
465 West End Avenue
New York, New York 10023
(212) 622-4802

PERSONAL

Date of Birth - March 31, 1948
Citizenship   - Algeria
Height   - 5'3"
Weight   - 130 lbs.
U.S. Work Permit issued 7/73

OBJECTIVE

Full-time employment as clerk-typist or typist-receptionist in New York firm.

EXPERIENCE

June 1973-
present

Clerk-typist, Jorgensen International, Carteret, N.J. Type data on office forms, file records, provide general office assistance.

EDUCATION

1971-1972 -

Attended Water Valley Junior College in Buffalo, N.Y. Earned A.A. in English Composition, May, 1972.

OFFICE SKILLS

Typing - 50 wpm
Filing

INTERESTS

Charcoal drawing, embroidery, ballet.

REFERENCES

Will be provided upon request.

PAUL RAYSON

(Confidential)

519 S. 4th Street
Edinburg, Texas 78539
Phone: Home: (512) 383-6655
Office: (512) 381-2515

OBJECTIVE

ADMINISTRATIVE STAFF

Research — Communication and Publications — Program Planning — Training

EXPERIENCE

1971 - present.   **Assistant Professor** in Department of History, **Pan American University,** Edinburg, Texas.
Conducts classroom lectures, discussions, examinations; leads and coordinates seminars. Performs course design, involving research and organization. Serves on various committees—e.g., honors council and self-study committee for University reaccreditation—entailing research and writing activity. Handles diverse administrative duties, including coordination of inter-departmental honors program, supervision of research projects, student counseling and recruitment.

Efforts have been instrumental in upgrading awareness of students in areas pertinent to fields of study; in attracting new students to school and department; and in improving personal skills in communication.
Among accomplishments: Through course organization, coordinated library of visuals, and revised and modernized reading list, succeeded in revitalizing two honors courses which had suffered severe enrollment losses under predecessor. Through extensive independent research, formulated and implemented pioneering courses which have earned high standing among departmental offerings.

1968 - 1971. **Assistant Professor** at **Falls View College,** Falls View, Mississippi; following brief fill-in assignment *(earlier in 1968)* during emergency situation at West Chester College, West Chester, Pennsylvania.
Performed teaching, research, administrative and other functions similar to those above.
Previously, **Graduate & Undergraduate Student;** with concurrent employment *(1966 - 1968)* as **Library Technician** in information services for **Free Library of New York,** and as **Music Director** for church.

EDUCATION / PROFESSIONAL QUALIFICATIONS / LANGUAGES

Ph.D. and A.M. degrees in American Civilization, from University of Pennsylvania, Philadelphia. Recipient of Woodrow Wilson, University and Harrison Fellowships.

B.A. *(with honors)* in American Studies, State University of New York at Buffalo. Elected to Phi Beta Kappa.

Publications: Author of essay "Containing Communism: the Art of Getting Along," in *Reason;* and of book reviews in *American Quarterly.*

Languages: Essential fluency in French; also some Spanish.

PERSONAL DATA

Born, 23 September 1941. Height, 6'; weight, 155. Unmarried, no minor dependents. Will relocate and/or travel as right opportunity may require.

REFERENCES Will be furnished on request.

Contact: Michael Fernandez
Mgr., Technical Search
Career Blazers Agency, Inc.
500 Fifth Avenue
New York, N.Y. 10036
(212) 730-1575

RONALD MOSKOWITZ

BUSINESS EXPERIENCE:

9/73–2/80   Du Pont Chemicals as Customer Engineer: The primary function of this position was to service large-scale computer systems. This function was to be performed in such a way as to maintain a high level of customer satisfaction. The other functions of this job included: installation, discontinuance, engineering alterations, and various other customer and sales support functions. Some of the skills required by the customer engineer are: time & resource management, an ability to perform prescribed maintenance procedures, adherence to corporate policies, effective two-way communication, and technical resourcefulness.

H/W

CPUS: 370/135 370/138 370/145 370/148

PERIPHERALS: 1403, 2540, 2821, 3203, 3215, 3211, 3811, 3272, 3277, 3284, 3286, 3330, 3333, 3340, 3344, 3350, 3830, 3410, 3411, 3420, 3803, 3505, 3525. (I've also worked on other CPUS from time to time, 1443 to 3800, 1419–3890 and a whole list of other I/O).

EDUCATION: I had training in other areas, such as; communication skills, Customer Relations, and Account Management. I've had formal training in DOS and OS Operating System Environments. I've some training in "Assembler" Language. I've been trained and thoroughly familiar with system diagnostic programs; OZTSEP, FRIEND, ST370 EREP, SEREP and CP-EREP.

United Electronics Institute; two year technical degree. Graduate in 1973

University of Colorado, 30 hrs, toward a B.S. in management.

Samuel J. Taylor
300 Riverside Drive
New York, New York 10025

212-797-3149

Date of Birth: December 1, 1946
Height: 6', Weight: 190
Marital Status: Married

RESUME CAPSULE:

Four years' experience as copywriter for leading publisher, as well as free-lance writing of film reviews over the past five years.

EXPERIENCE:

May 1972-
Present

Copywriter, Curtis-Hall, Inc., Publishers, Bergenville, New Jersey. Create and write advertising for direct-mail for premium sales and professional books; do layouts, designs and paste-ups for cover material; train new copywriters; condense copy from full-size publications into "mini" books for premium sales.

September 1970-
Present

Free-lance Film Reviewer, for various news media. Write reviews on educational films for radio and newspaper presentation.

EDUCATION:

B.A., June 1969, Cornell University.
M.F.A., June 1971, New York University.

SPECIAL HONORS

Phi Beta Kappa
Smithsonia Scholarship Award - 1967 and 1968.

HOBBIES AND INTERESTS

Collect fossils and seashells, scuba dive, sail, water ski.

REFERENCES

Will be furnished upon request.

COPYWRITER (SENIOR)/ADMINISTRATOR

CHRISTINA KAYE
40 Kalmbach Road
New City, New York   10956
(914) 222-3596

Born June 10, 1944
Height 5'3"
Weight 115 lbs.

RESUME CAPSULE: Four years' experience as Copy Chief for leading sales
agency, two years as Copy Chief and Senior Copywriter
as well as several years of free-lance work for major
producers of cosmetics, athletic organizations and
advertising firms.

EXPERIENCE

October 1969-
April 1979

Copy Chief, Martin Bruckner Agency, New York City.
In charge of selection, execution and all presentation
of promotional sales material, for all accounts
including leading cosmetic, lingerie, knitted garments,
and linen manufacturers.

May 1968-
September 1969

Senior Copywriter, Panels Unlimited, New York City.
Sales promotion ads and literature to trade, consumer
ads, and industrial copy.

June 1966-
April 1968

Assistant Copy Chief, Allied Radio, New York City.
Sales promotion, direct mail, trade and catalog copy,
consumer ads for all departments. Responsible for
special cooperative advertising with producers such
as Goldenrod Ceramics, Cornucopia Stoneware and Devon
Cosmetics.

September 1964-
May 1966

Copy/Marketing Trainee, McCabe Advertising, Inc., New
York City. Received training in all phases of copywriting/
marketing.

EDUCATION

B.B.A., June 1964, Pace Institute.

Graduate Work in Sociology, Advanced School of Social Research, Staten Island,
New York, September 1964-1966.

Executive Training Program, McCabe Advertising, September 1964-May 1966.

REFERENCES

Will be furnished upon request.

CREDIT MANAGER

MALCOLM LIDDY
290 West 11th Street
New York, New York 10014
212-243-5022

PERSONAL

Date of Birth: April 22, 1930
Military: U.S. Navy, Honorable Discharge 1953
Marital Status: Married, three children (adults)

BUSINESS EXPERIENCE

1958-1979   Credit Manager, Bonanza Adhesives, Inc., Milwau-
                   kee, Wisconsin. One of the nation's largest
                   producers of adhesive-backed products (labels,
                   tapes, etc.). Established all credit and collec-
                   tion systems, developed accounts receivable and
                   collections systems. Conducted credit analysis,
                   followed up all collections. Managed credit and
                   collection staff, personally reviewed all major
                   accounts and adjusted ratings. Periodically
                   reviewed and improved upon collections procedures.

1954-1958   Credit Accountant, North American Bank, N.Y.
                   Served as assistant to loan review supervisor.
                   All phases of credit appraisal, discounting of
                   commercial papers, handling of insolvencies.

EDUCATION

B.S. - 1951 - New York University. Majored in accounting and
business law, with Minor in banking and finance.

INTERESTS

Active in Little League, Community Chest, and other civic projects.

REFERENCES

Will be furnished upon request.

DESIGNER

Jerry Korban
345 Brighton Avenue
West New York, New Jersey 07093
Telephone: (201) 965-9845

Born: January 9, 1947
Height: 6'2"
Weight: 205 lbs.
Marital Status: Single

Work Experience:

Hazen and Sawyer, Engineers
360 Lexington Avenue
New York, New York 10017 (212) 986-0033

Work performed: trusted to solve unique problems throughout firm. Developed and negotiated with vendors of furniture, instruments (cameras, calculators, overhead pro-
jectors, etc.), stationery, and local and long-distance
messenger services; supervised in-house mailroom and
duplicating services. Designed covers; dealt with
typographers, printers, and word processing suppliers;
supervised production of reports and proposals. Responsible for office maintenance; dealt with building maintenance crew and outside firms; organized work parties for
files reduction program; organized filing system; controlled 1100 drawings for a $43,000,000 project.
Handled interviews for clerical staff; organized parties
and seminars; performed library and media research as
required.
November 1974 to March 1979

Raventos International Corporation
150 Fifth Avenue
New York, New York 10011 (212) 924-2490

Work performed: marketed an architectural service that
renovated, designed and constructed church buildings;
did writing and layout of brochures; wrote research reports
on current developments in liturgy and architecture.
Supervisor: Regina Rodda
June 1972 - September 1974

Fort Worth Community Theatre
Fort Worth, Texas

Work performed: acting, stage managing, set building,
lights, sound and publicity.
Supervisor: Jack Ellis
September 1971 to May 1972

Education:

Currently enrolled in Master of Urban Planning
program at NYU.

State University of New York at Stony Brook
Stony Brook, New York
B.A. English
Graduated: 1970

78

DIETITIAN

ROSETTA DEL'ORIFICE
2109 Broadway
New York, New York 10023
212-787-3200

Date of Birth: May 6, 1951
5' 6", 124 lbs.
Marital Status: Single

JOB OBJECTIVE: Position with food processor as staff
                  specialist.

EXPERIENCE

1971-1979   **Assistant Dietitian (part-time)**, Food Services
             Department, Masonic Temple, Detroit, Michigan.
             Helped plan menus and supervised preparation of
             all meals.

Summers   **Assistant to Chief Dietitian**, Marlboro State
1971-1973   Hospital, Marlboro, Michigan. Helped translate
             convalescent diets into actual meals, selected
             and delivered special meals to diet patients.

EDUCATION

B.S. degree, Michigan State University 1973. Nutrition Major.
Graduate courses on Environmental Effect on Man and His Menu,
Special Food for the Elderly, and Food Chemistry.

These courses provided an excellent background in elements of
nutrition as related to ecology, problems of the elderly, and
commercial food processing.

HONORS

Dean's List throughout four years of college.

SPECIAL INTERESTS

Gourmet cooking, camping, hiking.

REFERENCES

Will be furnished upon request.

Brian Mitchell
26 Court Street
San Francisco, California 94165
(415) 822-5621

Objective: To continue a career as a Medical Director in a large corporation; seeking to relocate in the southeast.

Experience:

1960 – present

Medical Director, Acem Elevator Co., San Francisco, California. Supervise all medical activities and am responsible for staff of three doctors, twelve nurses, three lab technicians and two secretaries. Supervise entire medical program: physical examinations, blood tests, medical emergencies, administration of flu school programs. Set up employee health plans. Liaison with insurance companies and Workmen's Compensation.

1951 – 1960

Physician, Hill & Hill, Inc., Los Angeles, California. Conducted physical examinations, treated injuries, handled medical emergencies. Administered Workmen's Compensation.

Education:

1950   Internship — Ithaca Hospital, Ithaca, New York.

1949   Doctor of Medicine, Cornell Medical School, Ithaca, New York.

1945   B.S. — Cornell University, Ithaca, New York.

Personal: Born: 8/1/27   Marital Status: Married
Height: 6' 1"   Weight: 215 lb.

References on request.

DRAFTER

ALBERTO ROSSI
One Top Stone Drive
Toledo, Ohio   43614
(419) 361-7444

OBJECTIVE: To serve as draftsman in supervisory capacity
              with manufacturer of mechanical or electrical
              products.

EXPERIENCE
1964-present   **Supervising Draftsman**, Toledo Castings, Inc.
               Toledo, Ohio. Implement engineering designs
               of pipes and fittings into working plans.
               Work with both synthetic fibre and cast iron
               pipes and fittings. Examine and give recom-
               mendations on cost, durability, and feasi-
               bility of production designs.

1959-1964   **Senior Draftsman**, Fire Engine Division,
               Supreme Truck Manufacturers, Romulus, N.Y.
               Assisted Senior Draftsmen in designing basic
               parts of mountings placed on truck chassis in
               constructing fire engines. Position provided
               invaluable training in gross and detailed
               design and first-hand work with engineers and
               craftsmen.

EDUCATION
   Certificate in Mechanical Drafting, Greenfield Trade School,
   Greenfield, New York - 1955.

MILITARY
   U.S. Army, 1956-1959. Staff Sergeant, Corps of Engineers.
   In addition to military training in drafting of bridges,
   roads, etc., took course in electronic drafting given by
   Ordnance Department on completion of active duty.

PERSONAL
      Date of Birth - June 3, 1937
      6 feet tall, 175 pounds
      Married, 1 child

REFERENCES
   Will be furnished upon request.

EDITOR

RÉSUMÉ

NAME: Thomas Wolfson

BUSINESS ADDRESS AND TELEPHONE NUMBER: Coolidge Institution on War, Revolution
    and Peace, Stanford University, Stanford, California 94305; 617-734-2979

HOME ADDRESS: 209 Southside Street, Springton, California 90916

DATE AND PLACE OF BIRTH: July 9, 1945; Shaketon, Missouri.

MARITAL STATUS: Single

FIELDS OF STUDY: History   Political Science (outside field)
                  Russia since 1500 (major)   Soviet Foreign Policy
                  Eastern Europe since 1453   International Communism
                  Western Europe since 1789   Marxist Theory

FOREIGN LANGUAGES: Russian (active knowledge)
                    French (active knowledge)
                    German (passive knowledge)

FELLOWSHIPS: Teaching Assistantship, Indiana University, 1968-69, 1969-70
              Graduate Assistantship, Indiana University, 1970-71, 1971-72
              Doctoral Student Grant-in-Aid for Research, Indiana University,
              1972-73

DISSERTATION: Rebuilding the Russian Army, 1909-14: A Study in the Formation
    of Policy under Nicholas II

CURRENT POSITION: Information Editor, Hoover Institution, 1969-present.

RESPONSIBILITIES OF CURRENT POSITION: Primary responsibilities are those of
    Assistant Editor of the Russian Review, a scholarly journal sponsored
    by the Hoover Institution. Read and evaluate incoming manuscripts, edit
    accepted manuscripts (both for content and for style), correspond with
    authors, undertake basic bibliographic research related to accepted manu-
    scripts, proofread at all stages of publication, assign new books to
    reviewers in appropriate fields, and secure necessary copyrights.

CAREER GOALS: Would like to work with a press interested in publishing scholar-
    ly books. Feel my broad liberal arts background provides a good frame of
    reference for reading and evaluating manuscripts submitted for publication.
    Having learned the basics of editing on the staff of a specialized quarter-
    ly, now desire to move to a position with broader scope and more potential
    for development and advancement.

EDUCATION: Ph.D. (major: history), 1977 (expected), Indiana University
             M.A. (major: history), 1969, Indiana University, Bloomington,
             Indiana
             A.B. (major: history), 1967, Duke University, Durham, North
             Carolina

REFERENCES: On request.

EDITOR (HISTORY BOOKS)

Gilbert G. Crossens
482 East 46th Street
New York, New York 10017

212-462-0934

OBJECTIVE   To apply background and interest in History to
               editing educational books on Early American History.

EXPERIENCE

  1973-1979   Instructor, Montveil Seminary, Montveil,
                 Pennsylvania. Principles of Economics, Early
                 American History, History of Economic Thought.

  1971-1972   Instructor, St. Agnes Convent, Convent Station,
                 N.J. Comparative Economic Systems, U.S.
                 Government, U.S. History.

  1970-1971   Instructor, Midvale College, Brooklyn. Economic
                 Institutions, American History.

  1969-1970   Editor, The World Today, Historical Society of
                 Philadelphia. Edited encyclopedia commentaries
                 on current events, particularly related to
                 American Politics and Historical Events.

EDUCATION
  Ph.D., Economics, Pennsylvania State University - 1974
  M.A., History, Pennsylvania State University - 1968
  B.A., Economics/History, Fordham College, New Jersey - 1965

PERSONAL DATA
American Citizen
Born September 12, 1945
Military Service - U.S. Army, 1965-67
Marital Status - Single

INTERESTS
  Piano, guitar, reading, writing science fiction.

REFERENCES
  Available on request.

EDITOR (SENIOR)

JOHN W. BOSITINO
2109 Broadway
New York, New York 10023
212 SU 7-2200

OBJECTIVE: To obtain position as Senior Editor with publisher of high
            school/college texts, general trade.

EXPERIENCE

11/69-6/78   Editor, Brace Publishing Corporation, New York, N.Y.
             Assisted the editorial director in reviewing and selecting
             general trade and business education titles, establishing
             publishing priorities, scheduling. Extensive author guidance
             in developing and refining manuscripts. Supervised free-
             lance design and editing. Some basic book design.

2/66-11/69   Senior Editing Supervisor, Pitt Division, Hill-Grenier Book
             Company, New York, N.Y. Manuscript review, editing, produc-
             tion control to bound books. Feature writing, revisions.
             Thorough training in layout and design.

9/64-2/66   Production Editor, Glen Publishing Company, Knoxville,
             Pennsylvania. All foreign language books, both hardbound
             and paperback. Supervision of freelance and in-house
             copyediting. Close work with authors, artists, designers.
             At least twenty-five titles per year.

7/62-9/64   Staff Editor, Alan Wilson & Sons, Inc., New York, N.Y.
             Copyediting in civil and electrical engineering, mathematics,
             biology, physics, economics, programming.

EDUCATION

M.A., English Literature/Linguistics, June, 1969, New York University, Graduate
School of Arts and Sciences.

B.A. (Majors in English and Spanish), June 1958, Winchester College, Milton,
New York.

PERSONAL DATA

Birth Date: May 28, 1936
Marital Status: Single
6'3", 199 lbs.

REFERENCES

Will be furnished upon request.

84

ELECTRONICS ENGINEER

Dennis Wong
256 Hill Street
San Francisco, California 94165
Phone 415 324-8461

Experience:

5/68
2/79

Apex Telephone, Inc., San Francisco, CA

Senior Marketing Engineer for both active
and passive electronic components. Serviced
Australian government and original equipment
manufacturers.

1/60
3/68

Spero Missiles, Carmen, CA

Senior Systems Integration Engineer, responsible for the complete integration of the
"Black Box" electrical sub-system of the
Polaris Missile into the entire weapon
system utilizing coordination drawings.

8/52
10/59

Northeast Telephone Laboratories, New York, NY

Member of the Technical Staff responsible for
the analysis of both wire-spring and reed-
spring relays as well as mechanical switches.
Assistant Project Engineer on the development
of electronic telephone equipment: e.g., push-
button dialing, direct distance dialing, and
solid-state ringers.

Education:

1946-
1952

MIT, B.S. and M.S. in Electrical Engineering

Date of birth: 2/14/29
Height: 5'6"
Weight: 138 lbs.
Marital Status: Married, 3 children

MARK BERGER
15 OVERLOOK DRIVE
CLIFTON, NEW JERSEY 07815
(201) 776-4232

PROFESSIONAL EXPERIENCE:

March 1974 - present

CARNEY, INC., CLIFTON, NEW JERSEY
Manager of Logistics at the Corporate Transportation/
Physical Distribution Division. Responsibilities
include systems analysis, logistic planning, facilities design, development and implementation of major
improvement projects; specialize in the areas of
cost reduction and analytical statistics.

February 1973 - February 1974

AGAR ALUMINUM, TEL AVIV, ISRAEL
Project Engineer. Responsibilities include
production control, methods, cost benefit analysis, and supervision of projects through all
phases of production.

January 1972 - February 1973

BARKER'S INSTRUMENTS, INC., NYACK, NEW YORK
Apprenticeship program specializing in production
of high precision components for the aerospace
industry utilizing computerized Numerical Control
equipment.

EDUCATION:

NEW YORK UNIVERSITY, NEW YORK, NEW YORK
M.S. in Industrial Engineering and Operation
Research, 1973

"TECHNION" - Tel Aviv Institute of Technology
B.S. in Industrial Engineering and Computer
Science, 1966-1970

SPECIALTIES:

Computer Science and Operation Research with respect
to production planning, systems analysis, system design
and management controls, using computer applications
and simulation techniques.

OBJECTIVES:

To engage in an established and highly sophisticated
Engineering/Management Department where there is an
opportunity for potential development and growth.

PERSONAL DATA:

Birthdate: 4/10/45. Marital Status: Married.
Draft Status: 1962-1965 Israeli Military Force.
Captain in Tank Force, in command of a Company.
Responsibilities included complete health and welfare,
limited strategic decision making, complete main-
tenance of tanks, equipment and guns.

References on request.

EXECUTIVE SECRETARY

LORRAINE HOFFMAN
56-26 121st Street
Cambria Heights, New York 11411   Telephone: (212) 693-3369

BUSINESS EXPERIENCE

September 1968-present

Executive Secretary to Research Director, Carter Baron Research Center, New York, N.Y. Handle personal and business correspondence, business records; make travel arrangements, maintain travel schedules; prepare and edit technical literature, catalogs, promotional brochures; arrange for placement of advertisements and notices in scientific journals; assist in the design and construction of several traveling displays for educational seminars and conventions on annual basis; attend these seminars to assist in promotional programs and presentations.

February 1967-August 1968

Executive Secretary, Baker Johnson Company, Brooklyn, New York. Executive secretary to President and Vice President of this small public relations company; acted as liaison between several account managers and sales representatives of client companies; set up conferences and presentations for prospective clients; maintained schedules.

May 1964-February 1967

Dictaphone Secretary, Gibbs Importers, Queens, New York. Transcribed correspondence, bills of lading, contracts, all necessary documents involved in receiving imported merchandise for distribution to stores.

EDUCATIONAL BACKGROUND

B.A., June 1969, Columbia University, New York
Major: English Literature

PERSONAL DATA

Date of Birth: February 6, 1945
Marital Status: Single

INTERESTS

Opera, ballroom dancing, tennis and golf

REFERENCES

Will be furnished upon request

FINANCE MANAGER

Mario Pesiri
859 Hobart Street
San Francisco, California 94110
(415) 875-0922

Age: 25
Married
No Children

Objective: To secure a responsible position in Financial Management with potential for challenge and fulfillment.

Education:
1974–1976
Stanford University, Stanford, California
Graduate School of Business Administration
September 1976 — Currently enrolled in second year electives in finance. President and founder of the Stanford Finance Club. Member of the Committee on Placement Services.

1970–1974
Stanford University
Degree: B.A. — Cum Laude, Political Science, Economics
January 1974 — Elected to Pi Sigma Alpha (Political Science Honor Society) and participated in intercollegiate athletics (Co-captain, Varsity Wrestling).

Experience:
9/75–present
Kidder, Peabody and Co., Inc., San Francisco, California
Intern — Internship in Financial Accounting and Treasury. Activities participated in are standard accounting, budgeting process, variance analysis, credit approval, management of bank balances and short-term money management. Furthermore, while in Treasury participated in activities related to city's tender offer.

5/74–9/75
United California Bank, San Francisco, California
Administrative Trainee assigned to Commercial Loan.
Responsibilities were to provide financial data to Commercial Account Officers, control and correct accounts held within the Automated Financial System. Principal accomplishments were the institution of procedures and controls, with respect to United California's Education Assistance Program, and the collection of arrears.

Summer and part-time employment with: San Francisco Public Library, St. Peter's Hospital, Woolworth and Company, and El Rancho.

Personal Data: Active in school and community welfare. Currently Director of the Mill Valley Recreational Wrestling Program. Active in church affairs with wife. Special interests include camping and woodworking.

References: Furnished upon request.

FINANCE TRAINEE / RECENT COLLEGE GRADUATE

Kevin M. Burk
412 Fernwood Street
Floral Park, New York 11047
(212) FL7-9872

Objective: To obtain a challenging position in the area of finance.

Education: Saint John's University, Jamaica, New York
Graduate School of Business Administration
Degree: M.B.A., August 1976
Concentration: Finance
Grade Average: 3.3 (4=A)

Manhattan College, Riverdale, New York
Degree: B.S., 6/75
Double Major: Economics and Biology

Experience: Four Corners Inn, Glen Oaks, New York
Cook and bartender; presently a 15-hour week.

1/76 Fischer's Motors, New Hyde Park, New York
Worked under the controller in improving the inventory
system.

7/75-11/75 Pinewood Bar and Grill, Riverdale, New York
Bartender.

6/75 Cohen's Transport Service, Bronx, New York
Delivered U.S. mail to post offices from a distribution
center before classes.

Summer 1974 Penn Central Railroad, New York, New York
Crossing watchman and track gang.

1971-1973
Summers Nuzzi Contractors, Floral Park, New York
Truck and container maintenance.

**Extracurricular
Activities:** Resident Advisor; Varsity Soccer Captain; Fraternity Social
Chairman; Initiator of College Spring Soccer Program; Member
of Omicron Delta Kappa - national honorary.

**Personal
Data:** Height 5'8"; Weight 145 lbs.; Age 23; Single; Willing to
relocate.

Background: Have lived in the New York area for over 20 years. Interests
include tennis, skiing, sailing, and music.

References: Available upon request.

89

FINANCE TRAINEE

Jose L. Hernandez
R.D. 143
Rutherford, New Jersey 07299
(201) 966-4985

Objective: To obtain a position as Investment Analyst.

Education:
6/75-8/76

Rutherford State College, Rutherford, New Jersey
Graduate School of Business Administration
Degree: M.B.A.
Graduated: August, 1976

Seton College, Newark, New Jersey
Degree: B.A.
Graduated: May, 1975
Concentration: History/Economics

Experience:
7/73-5/78

American Motor Credit Corporation, Port Jervis, New York
Presented finance packages (equity and lease) to retail
customers of truck, farm, and construction equipment.
Trained salesman of franchised dealerships in the presentation of finance plans. Handled retail collections and
repossessions.

1/70-11/71

Brown's Motor Acceptance Corporation, Newark, New Jersey
Conducted wholesale audits, retail collections and
repossessions.

6/69-1/70

Friendly Finance Corporation, Union, New Jersey
Conducted interviews of potential customers; handled retail
collections.

9/68-6/69

Kodak Corporation, Hackensack, New Jersey
Chemical Operator.

3/67-8/68

Volkswagon Parts Division, Ramsey, New Jersey
Materials Handler.

Military:
12/63-12/66

U.S. Army
PFC Infantryman; stationed in Okinawa for 31 months.

Personal:

Age: 29
Height: 5'9"
Weight: 190 lbs.
Health: Excellent
Married - 2 Children
Born in Newark, New Jersey

References: Furnished upon request.

FINANCIAL ANALYST

Gerald H. Stengel
24 West 65th Street
Brooklyn, New York
(212) 778-5901

EMPLOYMENT RECORD:

1971 - To Present   Manage Short-Term portfolio for Raleigh Insurance Co.
and subsidiaries, liaison with banks and dealers.
Manage New York Office.

1969-70   Commercial Paper Salesman - L.S. Martin and Company

1955-69   Commercial Paper Salesman - D.D. Stern and Company
Montreal

Activities included extensive dealings in selling
Commercial Paper and related money market instruments.
Negotiations involved corporations in Canada and the
United States. In addition to supervision and maintenance of existing markets, have a proven record for
the development and establishment of numerous new money
market instruments. Experience facilitated a substantial knowledge of United States and Canadian securities
and financial markets.

EDUCATION:

Graduated Ohio State University, B.A. Graduated Marietta
College Business School specializing in general business
practices, with emphasis on accounting.

POSITION OBJECTIVE:

Seeks a challenging and responsible position on the
staff of a large progressive corporation where vast
experience in short-term money market may be utilized;
or seeks affiliation with a brokerage house dealing in
activities of the money market.
Position should provide an atmosphere conducive to
professional growth and achievement, and one where
initiative will be welcomed.

SUMMARY OF QUALIFICATIONS:

Over 19 years of diversified practical experience dealing
in the following vital categories:

"Make Markets" in Commercial Paper. . . Bankers
Acceptances . . . Treasury Bills. . . in both U.S. and
Canadian markets. Offers excellent leadership quali-
ties combined with ingenuity and flexibility, proven

(Continued)

ability to pioneer in new techniques and projects, culminating in outstanding success. Coordinates and communicates effectively at all levels, and experienced in applying principles of good management in motivating maximum performance and efficiency among subordinate personnel.

PERSONAL DATA:

Born: 6/2/36
Marital Status: Divorced
Area of Preference: New York metropolitan area

References available on request.

FINANCIAL ANALYST/ RECENT COLLEGE GRADUATE

John M. Anderson

303 Front Street
Minneapolis, Minnesota 55437
(612) 445-9861

Date of Birth: 1/7/47
Marital Status: Married
Children: One

Position Desired: Financial Analyst, Accountant

Education:

6/74-6/76
Princeton University, Princeton, New Jersey
Graduate School of Business
Degree: M.B.A.
Concentration: Accounting

9/65-6/69
University of Maryland, Wilmington, Maryland
Degree: B.A., Biological Sciences
Minors: Chemistry, Education

Experience:

1/76-2/79
Dow Chemical Corporation, Princeton, New Jersey
Inventory accountant (during intercession)

6/74 - now
The Little Shack, Princeton, New Jersey
Night manager (52 hours/week concurrently with school)

9/72-1/74
U.S. Marine Corps, San Diego, California
Active duty, cost management analysis

4/70 -
Marine Reserve, Fort Hill Reserve Station, New Jersey

9/69-8/72
Orange County School District, Hackensack, New Jersey
Science teacher

Achievements
and Interests:
Member, executive council Beta Beta Beta Honorary
Society

Supervisor-trainer, military cost accounting and data
processing section; trained handicapped

Working knowledge of three computer languages

Marine unit and base advisory councils

Assistant coach of secondary school and college track
and country teams

Compete and officiate at track and field events and
county recreation programs

References: Furnished upon request

FINANCIAL ANALYST

JASON PARKER LOGAN
Two Connecticut Avenue
Menlo Park, California 94025
(415) 677-8834

PERSONAL DATA: Birthdate: 7/7/43
Weight: 170 lbs.
Height: 5'11"
Marital
Status: Married

EXPERIENCE:

Financial Planning and Analysis

Responsible for preparation of all quarterly and annual production and financial forecasts. Designed simulation model currently used to prepare divisional macro-economic forecasts, reducing forecasting time by 80% while improving timeliness and accuracy. Increased fourfold the number of corporate operating departments using these forecast data.

Atex Data Research, Greenwood, California 95635. 1973 - Present

Product Costing and Development

Directly responsible for preparation of all product cost forecasts. Develop corporate pricing policy and supporting economic justifications required by government regulatory agencies. Determine optimal intra-divisional allocation of resources. Improved costing techniques have significantly enhanced the competitiveness of product pricing.

Markham & Assoc., Stamford, Connecticut 06903. 1968 - 1973

Statistical Analysis

Developed and maintained detailed library of divisional operating statistics. Provided senior management with monthly and year-to-date comparisons of business results and financial forecasting information.

Business Sales Inc., Bridgeport, Connecticut 06605. 1965 - 1968

Marketing Planning

Tested revenue/expense impact of specific marketing strategy changes. Appointed internal marketing planning consultant to major mideast corporation (Saudia) reporting to Board of Directors.

Mideast Data Inc., Stamford, Connecticut 06902. 1963 - 1965

EDUCATION: M.A., Columbia University, New York, New York 10027. 1967
              B.A., UCLA, Los Angeles, California 90024. 1962

OBJECTIVE: Position in economic/business planning with a major financial
              institution affording an opportunity for advancement based on
              achievement.

References available upon request.

GRAPHICS COMPOSITION SPECIALIST

Janice Ann Halliday
3487 Peace Grove Drive
Atlanta, Georgia 30341

Telephone: (404) 321-4573

Born: December 12, 1952
Single
5'9'' / 118 lbs.

JOB GOAL   Graphics Composition Specialist

EXPERIENCE
1974-1979

Georgia Pacific Insurance, Atlanta, Georgia
Graphics Specialist

Handled work assignments that included statistical reports, booklets, brochures, manuals, slides, and promotional materials. Operated magnetic tape selectric composer system, as well as the electronic standalone composer, in the preparation of layout work which varied from rough draft materials to more complex layouts. Used drawing pen for line work of all kinds. Work required the use of judgment in copy marking and entering format instructions into the system output and in determining appropriate spacing and finished layout.

1971-1974

Murray Wood and Paper Company, Atlanta, Georgia
Statistical Typist/MT/ST Operator

Typed a variety of statistical reports, sales forecasts, and charts. Received special training on MT/ST, Composer and MT/SC equipment and the drawing pen. Acquired knowledge of type designs and layout fundamentals during a period of two years as a trainee and then as a specialist.

1969-1971

Georgia Power and Light Company, Atlanta, Georgia
Clerk Typist

Typed invoices, performed routine clerical tasks and maintained files. Typed from copy and developed statistical skills. Typed charts and statistics for the annual report to stockholders.

EDUCATION

1969 — Certified at Woods Business School
1968 — Graduated from Lee High School

References on request.

HOSPITAL ADMINISTRATOR

ERIC JORGENSEN
555 Middlevale Avenue
Middlevale, New York 13406
716-828-1132

PERSONAL

Date of Birth: February 21, 1942
Marital Status: Married, 2 children
6'2", 190 lbs.

OBJECTIVE

To serve as Chief Administrator
of rural general hospital.

EXPERIENCE

1971-1979   Chief Administrator, Riverdale General Hospital,
                 Riverdale, Montana. Directed all administrative
                 functions of this 250-bed hospital. Established
                 all policies, supervised operation of administra-
                 tive departments (with three assistant administra-
                 tors). Supervised both professional and non-
                 professional personnel, budgeting, special projects,
                 training logistics. Represented the hospital in
                 all community affairs and health activities.

1969-1971   Hospital Administrator, Chelsea General Hospital,
                 Chelsea, Ohio. Directed the activities of all
                 supervisors, developed more efficient admissions
                 procedures and developed a public relations-
                 oriented staff training program, and greatly
                 improved the overall atmosphere of the hospital
                 as well as its status in the vicinity.

1967-1969   Assistant Hospital Administrator, Bronx Military
                 Hospital, Bronx, Indiana. Conferred with Chief
                 Administrator on all phases of hospital administra-
                 tion, including patient admission procedures,
                 allocation of office and ward space; interviewed
                 and selected personnel, and in general had respon-
                 sibility for efficient operation in all departments
                 of this 200-bed hospital and all aspects of patient
                 comfort and rehabilitation.

EDUCATION

                 Master's degree in Hospital Administration, June
                 1966, Allentown Medical College, Allentown, Wiscon-
                 sin, with one-year administrative residence at
                 Levittown County Hospital in Allentown. (Continued)

ERIC JORGENSEN   Hospital Administrator

EDUCATION (cont'd.)

B.S. - 1963, Allentown University - Chemistry Major.

MILITARY BACKGROUND

1966-1967 - First Lieutenant, Medical Service Corps.

REFERENCES

Will be furnished upon request.

COSETTE LANDER

125 South 10th Street
Philadelphia, Pa. 19124
215/ 685-7941

Born: 9/18/46
Height: 5'8"
Weight: 136
Marital Status: Divorced,
1 child

Objective

Position as housekeeper/dietitian in
resort hotel or motel requiring supervisory ability and offering full
maintenance

Experience:

9/71 - present

Housekeeper/Dietitian Fulton House Motel,
Bala Cynwyd, Pa.

Direct staff of 40 porters and maids;
responsible for recruiting and supervising staff of summer college student
personnel; purchase all supplies and
equipment.

6/68 - 9/71

Dietitian Henry Hudson Hotel, Port Jervis,
N.Y.

Responsible for planning menus and supervising 5-person kitchen; functioned as
hostess and supervised 5 waiters and 4
busboys.

Education:

B.S. Cornell University, Ithaca, N.Y.
Major: Home Economics
Minor: English

References on request.

INSURANCE CLAIMS ADJUSTER

Paul Reynolds
25 Bayside Avenue
Seneca, New York 14547
(716) 493-9675

    Born 5/6/38; 6'2"; 210 pounds; married; no children

<u>Job Objective</u>	Supervisory position in insurance adjusting

Experience

7/71 - present   <u>Claims Adjuster</u>
National Insurance Company
Seneca, New York
Responsible for making on-the-scene investigations, obtaining statements from witnesses,
assessing property damage, determining liability
and negotiating settlement.

6/60 - 6/71   <u>Office Claims Representative</u>
Standard Insurance Company
Ithaca, New York
Duties included receiving claim forms, con-
firming coverage and issuing settlement draft.

7/58 - 5/60   <u>Property Damage Trainee</u>
Acme Casualty Company
Watkins Glen, New York
Duties included inspecting material damage,
obtaining photos, preparing property damage
estimates and obtaining agreed prices with
body repair shops.

Education

1956 - 1958   Laraby Junior College, Elmira, New York

<u>Hobbies</u>   Photography
Carpentry
Skiing

<u>References</u>   Available upon request.

INTERIOR DECORATOR

Jay Oliver   Home Phone: (512) 203-5681
685 Summer Street   Business Phone: (512) 986-2384
Austin, Texas 78745

Born: December 29, 1943   Height: 5'10"
Marital Status: Divorced   Weight: 170 pounds

Career Objective: Interior Decorator

Experience: Interior Decorator - J and B Decorators, Austin
6/70 - present   Texas
                       Client contact to determine decorating tastes
                       and choices for homes and apartments; submitted
                       sketches and color choices; responsible for
                       shopping, installing and supervising painters,
                       carpenters, etc.

1/65 - 5/70   Dispatcher - C.B. Temporaries, Austin, Texas
                       Interviewed applicants, took orders from client
                       companies, dispatched proper temporary to each
                       assignment, assisted in bookkeeping.

Education: University of Texas
1961-1965   B.A. Degree, Art Major

References: Available on request.

Patricia Jones
15 Cayaka Street
Los Angeles, California 90057
(213) 542-5625

Born: 1/1/37
Height: 5'4"
Weight: 120 lbs.
Marital Status: Married
Three Children

Experience:

2/66 - present   **Investigator**, J & J, Inc., Los Angeles, California. Function as field investigator to determine the underwriting acceptability for insurance companies, investigate prospective employees for client employers, interview claimants with regard to insurance claim. Dictate cases to secretarial pool.

8/55-2/66   **Inspector**, Los Angeles Credit Company, Los Angeles, California. Inspect property to be insured to ascertain that property is as stated in the insurance application; responsible for photographing and sketching such property.

Education:
1955

Los Angeles High School
Los Angeles, California

References: Available upon request.

KEYPUNCH OPERATOR

Judy Lee Foster
56 Highland Avenue
Louisville, Kentucky 40223
Telephone: (502) 498-8874

Date of Birth: 11/6/50
Height: 5'6"
Weight: 120 pounds
Married

Job Objective - Key Punch Supervisor

Experience

1973-1979   Key Punch Operator: Blue Grass Enterprises, Inc. - Louisville, Ky.

Worked under the direction of the Group Head transcribing data
from source documents to punched cards, following standardized
procedures and instructions. Learned to handle jobs without
specific instructions. Operated alphabetical and numerical
key punch and key verifier machines with speed and accuracy.
Located on the source document the items to be punched and often
had to decipher illegible ones and prepare new ones. Assisted
other operators who were in training.

1971-1973   Transcribing Machine Operator: Colonel Harvey Foods - Louisville,
Ky.

Typed a variety of recorded material, including complex, technical
and sometimes confidential reports. Required to make the proper
choice of layout and form and to be sure punctuation and grammar
were correct.

1969-1971   Clerk Typist: Turtle Manufacturing Company - Lexington, Ky.

Used dictaphone to type letters; typed reports from typewritten
drafts. Did some statistical typing and typed invoices and
purchase orders. Answered call director and helped receptionist.
Operated embossograph to cut name plates and used adding machine.

1968-1969   File Clerk: First National Bank - Lexington, Ky.

Arranged, sorted and filed invoices, correspondence and other
miscellaneous material. Retrieved and refiled items as requested.
Performed some typing assignments.

Education

Lexington Mason High School, Business Studies Diploma, 1968

References

Provided on request.

LABORATORY TECHNICIAN

Harry R. Leason
6789 Vander Drive
Lemon Grove, California 92045

(805) 657-8934

Date of Birth: 5-7-47
Married: 3 children
5'9" -- 155 lbs.
Will relocate

Job Objective: Senior Laboratory Technician

Experience

Skilled Technician
1969-1979

Ace-Hunt Pet Food Company, Fullerton, California

Carried out specialized, complex, non-repetitive experiments requiring extensive knowledge of the technology involved. Performed routine experiments, operated experimental equipment, and produced experimental samples of materials according to established quality standards. Assigned to lead a group of less experienced technicians (college recruits) in specific assignments. Communicated results of assignments within the established format.

Laboratory Technician
1967-1969

Performed varied routine tests required and prepared samples. Set up and operated laboratory equipment such as colorimeter, spectrophotometer, refractometer, microscopes, mixers, dryers, grinders, filters and the enlarging and contact apparatus for photographic work.

Laboratory Assistant
1965-1967

Worked under the supervision of the Group Leader performing simple chemical and physical test routines. Assisted in the assembly and set up of equipment; prepared standard test solutions and regimens; recorded test data; and as required, performed routine detailed work in the research and development laboratories as requested by the professional staff. Kept laboratory clean and in good order and handled and cared for small animals.

Education

Lemon Grove High School. Received diploma in 1965.

Won Lemon Grove Science Competition Award in 1963.

References

On request.

LIBRARIAN (CORPORATE)

Elizabeth R. Jonas
3450 Downer Road
Seattle, Washington 98116

Telephone: (206) 576-8934

Date of Birth: June 1, 1946

Height: 5'6" / Weight: 120 lbs.
Health: Excellent
Divorced/2 children

Job Objective: **Corporate Librarian**

Experience

1970—1979

Marketing Librarian
Oakland Electronics Corporation — Seattle, Washington

Maintain Marketing Library providing extensive source material for marketing personnel and a marketing information service to operating divisions. Issue a bulletin periodically listing new publications, articles and studies on marketing as well as competitive new products.

Research, summarize and submit comprehensive information on all areas related to the corporation's interests, from secondary sources and outside contacts. Keep statistical tables on population and socioeconomic trends, consumption and prices; other demographics. Maintain comprehensive and up-to-date information and constantly add to and update holdings.

Establish and maintain continuing relationships with sources of information (government bureaus, consulates of foreign countries, trade associations, trade and consumer press, special libraries, and public libraries) through phone calls, visits, correspondence and attendance at library association meetings.

1968—1970

Assistant Librarian
Holt, Wagner and Smith Investment Brokerage — Seattle, Washington

Scanned periodicals and referred specific articles to interested personnel. Clipped and filed items of permanent value. Cataloged books, maintained library files and revised when necessary, handled routine requests for material, and checked listings of new material in trade press, outside sources, and government bulletins. Ordered books, pamphlets, magazines as needed to keep the library collection updated.

Education

University of Oregon — B.S. degree Library Science — 1967

References

Will be provided on request.

MAIL SUPERINTENDENT

Henry O'Connor
145-96 Smart Street
Chicago, Illinois 44498
(315) 598-9987

Date of Birth: 5/6/39
Marital Status: Married
Height: 5'8"
Weight: 150 lbs.

Experience:

March 11, 1974
    to
  Present

Charles Booker, Inc.   Stock Brokerage
97 Lake Michigan Drive
Chicago, Illinois 44493

Currently Purchasing Manager responsible for office
supplies which include stationery, envelopes,
departmental forms, bank checks, etc.; printing,
all in-house and outside vender contracts; furniture and machines (i.e.,Pitney Bowes, UARCO,
Addressograph, Xerox and IBM); and all maintenance
contracts relating to the latter.

Responsibilities also include managing the Mail
Department which has a staff of eight. The Mail
Department handles all incoming and outgoing mail,
daily confirmations, monthly statements, printing
on a 1250 Multilith, UARCO disbursements and inventory control (Burster and Delever machines).

Through varied experience in purchasing and line
management, have implemented inventory control
procedures. Currently using manual forms to
control all levels of inventory. Current inventory
control procedures tie in purchasing, inventory
management, reordering surplus and equipment evaluation as a unique separate function. Have developed
contacts with outside venders and have initiated
blanket order contracts to create savings for the
firm.

December, 1963
    to
March 8, 1974

Blackman and Miller Co., Inc.   Stock Brokerage
48-07 Bank Street
Chicago, Illinois 44492

Duties were exactly the same as stated above. Firm
went into liquidation.

June, 1959
    to
December, 1963

Cassidy, Newman, Bright and Eli   Stock Brokerage
755 East 8th Street
Chicago, Illinois 44497

Duties were basically the same as stated above.

References: Will be supplied upon request.

MAILROOM SUPERVISOR

Cecil Cooke
387 Perry Street
Columbus, Ohio 43216
(614) 485-0052

EDUCATION

High School - Commercial Diploma

HONORS

Superior Accomplishment Award - United States Postal Service

BUSINESS BACKGROUND

Three and one-half years served in Army Air Force - 1st Lieutenant.
Thirteen years in Air Force reserve.

Thirty-four years with the United States Postal Service. Fourteen years
as Supervisor (middle line). Duties covered all aspects of mail service
including rules and regulations, rates, delivery, and processing. Bulk
mail and weighers mail supervisor. Received and processed heavy mailing and parcel post for commercial and non-profit organizations. Parcel
wrapping and mail binding knowledge.

Retirement - March 1, 1976

SPECIAL SKILLS

Knowledge of postal rates

PERSONAL DATA

Date of birth: 7/30/21
Height: 5'4" Weight: 130 lbs.

REFERENCES

Suitable business and personal references will be submitted upon
request.

Anthony S. Carlucci
7605 Bay 18th Street
Brooklyn, N.Y. 11238
Telephone (212) 456-6543

Objective
       A position offering an opportunity for growth using my
knowledge and experience in administrative management.

Business Experience (10/72-present)

       With Williams & Patterson, Inc., Supervisor - Mail
Services, Receiving, Microfilm Fileroom and Bookbinding
Departments (Corporate Headquarters). Responsibilities
include supervision of thirty employees, planning and
directing all phases of departmental operations, interviewing and reviewing all personnel, preparing work schedules,
coordination of all special projects (monthly statement
mailings, traffic analysis, mechanical mailing, etc.).

Education

       Management Techniques I - Williams & Patterson Training
       Department, 1973
       Supervisory Techniques - Williams & Patterson Training
       Department, 1975
       Operations Skills - Williams & Patterson Training Depart-
       ment, 1976

       Hunter College - Evenings, 1973
       Long Island University, 1969-1972 - History Major

Personal Data

       Date of Birth: May 5, 1952
       Marital Status: Single
       Height: 5'8"
       Weight: 135 lbs.
       Hobbies: Tennis, motorcycling, rock collecting. Served
       two terms as Student Government Representative in high
       school. Received "Honor Achievement" awards in Mathe-
       matics, History and Science. Served two years as Vice
       President, Pi Alpha Omega Fraternity while attending
       Long Island University. In addition, served one term
       as a Student Council Representative.

MANAGER (ADVERTISING AND SALES PROMOTION)

BRUCE CAMPBELL
2100 Broadway
New York, N.Y.   10023

212 SU 7-4210

OBJECTIVE: To relocate to suburban area with
position as Manager of Research or
Advertising in a small publishing
company.

EXPERIENCE

1973-Present   Manager, Advertising and Sales Promotion,
Carlton Publications, New York, N.Y. In charge
of all phases inherent in publication of six
trade magazines with nationwide distribution
to industrial corporations.

1972-1973   Manager, Advertising and Sales Promotion,
Collins Research Corporation, Bear Lake,
New York. Directed all operations involved
in advertising and sales promotion, with staff
of eight, in this company which produced electrical meters and various electrical components
used in radios and television sets.

1971-1972   Advertising Manager, Hersey-Starling Electronics
Division, New York, N.Y. Integrated and supervised activities involved in publicity and sales
promotion of products, including transistors,
receivers, television picture tubes, digital
display devices and digital integrated circuits.

1961-1971   Manager, Advertising and Sales Promotion, William
Meyers Associates, New York, N.Y. Organized and
executed advertising and sales presentation
programs for the promotion of this company's
products which included pipe fittings and meter
valves, thermostats and various control devices.

1950-1961   Valve Design Engineer, Marine Motors, Seagirt,
Long Island. Designed valves for use in marine
equipment. Conducted research for improvement
in design and construction of these valves.

(Continued)

Bruce Campbell   Manager, Advertising and
                                        Sales Promotion

EXPERIENCE (cont'd.)

1946-1950   Assistant Project Engineer, Cylinder Design Dept.,
                   Curtis Motor Design Corporation, Alison, New Jersey.
                   Made blueprints and sketches of original designs
                   for motor cylinders, for cars, trucks and tractors.
                   Investigated and corrected design imperfections in
                   cylinders already in operation in motor vehicles,
                   for more efficient functioning.

EDUCATION

   B.S. in Automotive Engineering, 1946 - Pace Polytechnic Institute

PUBLICATIONS

   Series of five articles on investigative research into the causes
   of malfunction, and correction of defective auto parts, published
   in *Automotive America,* January-May issues, 1974.

PERSONAL

Date of Birth: January 2, 1926
6 feet tall, 205 lbs.
Married, 3 children

REFERENCES

   References on request.

MANAGER (JUNIOR)

John Storms
12 Otto Place
Jalose, Arizona 86331
612 — 519-0612   Administration

Education

>   Lehman College, City University of N.Y., B.A. Cum Laude, June, 1973
>   Major: Economics
>   Minor: English
>
>   Honor: Omicron Delta Epsilon — National Economic Honor Society
>   Regents Scholarship
>   Intramural Tennis Champion

General Background

7/73-4/79   One year of special training and two years of subsequent work experience as an administrator and teacher for a nonprofit educational organization. Administrative duties required creative and intelligent thinking, as well as the ability to work closely with others in providing educational programs to the public, coordinating office activities and effecting successful public relations.

Employer: World Plan Executive Council
            National Center
            Pacific Palisades, Ca.

6/68-12/72   Prior work experience during student years consisted of tutoring economics, accounting and French, general bookstore work (sales, register, shipping, etc.) and summer employment as a counselor and waiter.

Skills

>   Typing 55 wpm

Personal Data

>   Born September 12, 1950   Height — 6'1"
>   Single   Weight — 175 lbs.

References

>   Available on request.

CARLETON K. ROBERTS
16 Bell Street
Harris, Minnesota 55941
Telephone: 218-583-9313

OBJECTIVE: Result- and profit-motivated innovative marketer with
accomplishments in Corporate Market and Economic Research,
Marketing Management Consulting, Market Development.
Target Corporate Development.

EXPERIENCE:

SENIOR MARKET
RESEARCH ANALYST   FAL CORPORATION, New Falls, Minnesota   1974-present

Responsible to the Manager of Market Research for collection
and analysis of information in business areas of interest
to the corporation. Survey and evaluate literature and
interpret trends where relevant. Organize investigations,
analyze, report findings and recommendations to management.

Recommended a course of action for establishing R&D objective.
Researched and developed a half billion dollar market
related to current product lines. Market segmentation pin-
pointed R&D goals.

Suggest market opportunities, consult on new products,
evaluate production and supply statistics. Interpret
economic news.

SENIOR ANALYST   JOHNSON AND CO., INC., Raleigh, S. Carolina 1966-1974

Engaged in all functional responsibilities necessary to
answering critical questions for Fortune 500 clients. Advanced from Market Analyst to Senior Associate. Developed
more than 50 major studies calculated to have yielded millions
of dollars to corporate customers.

Studies were sponsored to: audit and define consumer and
industrial markets; help plan and test new products and
services; evaluate sales and distribution operations;
appraise acquisitions or divestitures; plan production
facilities proximate to markets, etc.

(Continued)

Personal research has effectively:

-Evaluated the distributor network of a proposed 15 million dollar corporate acquisition.
-Determined the advisability of a client divesting a 10 million dollar sales division.
-Delineated the market for production of a proposed 19 million dollar turnkey process facility.
-Measured share of market and isolated areas for penetration for a 100 million dollar supplier of specialty materials.
-Developed statistical and qualitative audits of industries segmenting profitability of product markets. Used by sponsors to plan multi-million dollar productions and define goals.

FIELD UNDERWRITER   STATE INSURANCE, Greg Plains, Nebraska   1963-1966

Marketed personal lines of coverages. Trained and received New York State licensing. Conducted telephone and in-person prospecting. Sold concepts and underwrote life, health, and disability protection and/or to meet estate plans.

SALES MANAGER   FIELD BROS. IMPORTERS LTD., N.Y., N.Y.   1950-1963

Administered territorial sales and marketing activities. Successfully motivated the several forms of customers to stock and promote sales of a broad line of packaged goods. Cultivated associated distributor personnel's cooperation and gained their interest in promoting coverage and sales volume.

Achieved near saturation distribution in a market containing over 2,000 accounts. Was successful in converting this near virgin territory to a highly profitable market with improved volume of over 800%.

Projected company policies, sales supports and product uniqueness to the industry and in distributor meetings.

EDUCATION: B.B.A., Major Economics, University of Miami, Coral Gables, Florida.

PERSONAL: Married, 3 children. Born January 27, 1929.

REFERENCES: Available upon request.

MARKETING MANAGER

BARRY WESTIN
52-32 Sycamore Street
Forest Hills, New York   11375   212-345-6731

EXPERIENCE

1973-1979   Production Manager, Ronson Management Research, Inc.,
               New York City. P/L responsibility for $500,000
               marketing budget used in direct mail, space advertis-
               ing and telephone sales. Wrote annual marketing
               plans and forecasted product pro-forma statements.
               Doubled 1974 revenues to $1.6 million by segmenting
               existing markets and pinpointing new ones. Inte-
               grated marketing and financial data to rank markets
               according to profitability. Heavily used cost
               accounting and advanced marketing research techniques.
               Supervised copywriters, artists, printers and media
               buyers in advertising and sales promotion campaigns.

1971-1973   Marketing Research Analyst, Rolands Mail Order House,
               Milwaukee, Wisc. Developed statistical program for
               evaluating new customer credit applications. Used
               analysis of variance techniques to correlate customer
               demographics with payment history. Determined opti-
               mal mailing sequence for catalog and direct mail
               response. Determined user needs. Wrote MIS specifi-
               cations for corporate programming staff.

EDUCATION

1971-1973   Graduate School of Business, Milwaukee University,
               M.B.A. Concentrated in Marketing and Financial
               Management. Secondary interests in Organizational
               Development.

1965-1970   University of Detroit. B.S. degree.
               Majored in Systems Analysis Engineering and Opera-
               tions Research.

HONORS   Recipient of Astor Scholarship at Milwaukee
               University, and Michigan State and Morgansteiner
               Scholarships at University of Detroit. Graduated
               with honors.

LANGUAGES   Speak both French and German fluently.

PERSONAL   Married
               5'11", 165 lbs.
               Born May 2, 1949

INTERESTS   Tennis and long distance running.

MARKETING MANAGER

Travor Hill Johnson
214 Main Street
Charleston, West Virginia 25201
(304) 357-8075

23 years old
married, no children
female

Education: University of Chicago, Chicago, Illinois. Received M.B.A. in June, 1975. Work included four courses in marketing, including marketing management, family consumer behavior, market research and international marketing; financial and cost accounting; macroeconomics and microeconomics; investments; calculus; linear programming and statistics. M.B.A. work also provided experience with an interactive data analysis system in statistics and exposure to systems analysis and basic assembly language.

Union College, Schenectady, New York. Received B.A. in American Studies in June, 1973. Course work included sociology, history, economics, literature and psychology oriented to the study of American culture and group life. Senior Thesis on subject of the ideals of cooperation and competition in American educational thought. Involved in committee to strengthen American Studies program at Union. Dean's List. Completed course work in three years.

Work Experience:

February, 1976
to
present

The Commonwealth Group, Stamford, Connecticut. Consultant. Responsible for design and execution of marketing study for a Connecticut bank interested in the Stamford business community. Project includes internal and external interviews and extensive competitive analysis to arrive at a positioning for the bank and other recommendations about Stamford operations. Also involved in certain stages of new business activities and analysis of other consulting projects.

June to
September, 1975

AMF Alcort, Waterbury, Connecticut. Consultant. Gathered and interpreted statistical and other data related to the present and potential markets for the Sunfish sailboat to determine the product's annual sales potential nationwide. Worked with corporate, Marine Products Group and Alcort personnel.

Autumn, 1974

David Overton Associates, Barrington, Illinois. Consultant. Constructed cost model for the packaging, transportation and distribution of a consumer product on a regional basis. Involved in developing marketing plans for product. Work done on a consulting basis while in business school.

Summer, 1973

Alan Wood Steel, Conshohocken, Pennsylvania. Mill clerk in cold mill. Maintained production and other statistics.

Summer, 1970

Vocational Adjustment Center, South Boston, Mass. Work involved supervising retardates in behavior-modification setting.

IRENE C. NEWMEYER

HOME ADDRESS:
84-84 Dalny Road
Jamaica, New York   11432
(212) 523-1904

SCHOOL ADDRESS:
4309 Hortensia Avenue
San Diego, California   92103
(714) 297-9952

job
objective

A position offering challenge and responsibility in the realm
of consumer affairs, marketing or advertising research.

education

The University of California

1973-1977

Graduating in May 1977 with a B.A. Degree in MARKETING AND
CONSUMER BEHAVIOR. DEAN'S LIST DISTINCTION.
Fields of study include: marketing and advertising theory and
research, economics, business law, calculus, mass communications,
statistics, psychology, sociology, and research methodology.
BERKELEY COURSES: Social and Managerial Concepts in Marketing,
Consumer Behavior, Product Policy, Advertising Theory and
Policies, Sales Force Management, Marketing Research.
                  SENIOR RESEARCH SEMINARS AND PROJECTS:
        * * Children and Advertising
        * * Marketing Research - Cash vs. Credit Retail Analysis
        * * Portrayal of Women in Magazine Advertising (Role Model)
        * * Persuasive Impact of Liquor Ads in Print Media
        * * The Male Contraceptive Pill: Product Development and
                  Marketing Strategies, including Advertising
        * * INDEPENDENT STUDY ON ADVERTISING EFFECTIVENESS

1969-1973

John Adams High School - San Diego, California
National Honor Society, Senior Class President. Headed all fund-
raising programs for Senior Class.

work
experience
SUMMERS
1976

CALIFDATA CORPORATION - San Diego, California
Administrative assistant in Sales Department. Trained in basic
sales and organizational procedures. Responsible for record
keeping, expense reports, public relations, correspondence,
inventory updates, and billing.

1975

GRAHAM MILLS - La Jolla, California
Basic sales and management training. Responsible for billing,
orders, inventory maintenance, shipping arrangements, deliveries.

(Continued)

1974   THE PRESS CLUB (Office) - San Diego, California
          Extensive experience in inventory control, contracts, billing,
          correspondence and public relations.

extra-   Down South - responsible for soliciting advertisers as well as
curricular writing copy and layout for "Intro to California." Active with
activities Freshman Orientation Programs. UCSD Marketing and Management
           Club - involved with structuring innovative lecture series in
           career opportunities in related fields and designing community
           "Intern" Program. California Consumer Board - volunteer.

interests   people, theater, music, sailing, tennis, travel

personal   born: 8/13/55   marital status: single

references available on request.

MARKETING SALES DIRECTOR

Anthony T. Falk
569 59th Avenue
Tulsa, Oklahoma   74105

Telephone: (918) 529-3309

5 feet 11 inches; 160 pounds
Single
Date of Birth: September 1, 1939

Job Objective: Marketing/Sales Director

Experience   King Regan Corp., Tulsa, Oklahoma
1970-1979   Assistant to President

Directed the marketing for new products in the freeze-dried
field. Researched the market and competition, test-marketed
products and trained sales force for national distribution.
Followed the successful distribution of products on consumer
level with the training of institutional sales staff to open
key institutional accounts.

Found new markets for established products and opened
European distribution for U.S. products. Developed sales
and marketing strategy, searched for and identified specific
markets and developed methods of penetrating those markets.

Responsibility for advertising, packaging, promotions and
product development.

1968-1970   Crowley Industrial Bag Inc., Cleveland, Ohio
                  Marketing Director

Responsibility for diversification to consumer products,
opening key accounts, directing new technology. Utilized
market research methods, impact point of purchase pieces
and both product and corporate advertising to launch the
consumer products. Worked closely with package designers
to develop unified packaging with a hard-sell profile.
Supervised training of a special sales force.

1965-1968   Ace Marine Supplies and Boats, Chicago, Illinois
                  Product Manager

Created new markets for established products and recommended
product improvements. To capitalize on the growing demand
for fiber glass boats, worked with designers to make changes
in our 40-foot yacht to create a 40-foot motor sailboat.
The market followed our trend and sales more than doubled over
sales on the original yacht in the line in previous years.

(Continued)

1963-1965   Chicago Sun Times, Chicago, Illinois
                 Salesman
                 _____

                 Sold classified and display advertising in local market.

Education   1963 M.B.A. degree from University of Chicago.

                 Graduated 1960 from Xavier University with B.S. and B.A.
                 degrees in Economics and Accounting.

References   On request.

MEDIA MANAGER

ROGER W. MARKEY
291 West 78th Street
New York, N.Y. 10023
212-838-2210

JOB OBJECTIVE: To serve in the management area of a media
                   company.

EXPERIENCE

1974-1979   Administration Assistant, International Tobacco
                   Company, Kavalla, Greece.

1972-1974   District Manager for Circulation Department,
                   Intervale Newspapers, Inc., Roanoke, Virginia.
                   Reported to Circulation Manager, responsible
                   for the operation of thirty-nine retail routes.
                   Doubled sales quota in sales promotional program
                   leading the eighty-one outstanding districts.
                   Supervised District Managers in districts having
                   poor management problems.

1969-1972   Continued studies at Western Commonwealth
                   University.

1968-1969   Staff Member, Applied Physics Laboratory,
                   Sebastian Highlands, Florida. Staff member on
                   acoustical research boat based out of Florida.

1966-1968   Head of Administration, Mellon Enterprises.
                   Served as Head of Administration for Mellon
                   estate, Vero Beach, Florida.

EDUCATION

Business Administration and Economics Major at Western Commonwealth University, Roanoke, Virginia, 1964-1966, 1969-1972.

Graduated from Martha Washington High School, Roanoke, Virginia,
June 1964. Captain of indoor and outdoor track teams in junior
and senior years.

INTERESTS

Photography, Antiques, Ancient History.

PERSONAL

Born January 14, 1946
6', 180 lbs.
U.S. Citizen
Single

REFERENCES

Furnished upon request.

MEDIA PLANNER

ANDREW EASTON
10 Tyrolia Lane
Lawrence, N.Y. 11559

Home Phone: (516) 513-0791
Business: (516) 886-1169

BUSINESS HISTORY

TYLO AND TYLO, INC.

1968 - 1979 - Associate Media Director

> Prepared media plans for Lenox China, International Silver,
> Binney and Smith (Crayola), Loctite, Connecticut Bank and Trust
> Co., Julius Wile.

CONEDIA AND EVVON, INC.

1962 - 1968 - Media Buyer

> Prepared media plans and supervised media research. Handled
> buying on such accounts as Dutch Boy Paint, Hartford Insurance,
> Genesee Beer, Snow Crop and Chun King.

ESTHERSON ASSOCIATES

1951 - 1962 - Print Media Buyer and Media Specialist (Business Papers)

> Prepared media plans and recommendations on magazines, newspapers,
> and business papers for specific accounts including Continental
> Can, Armstrong Cork, U.S. Steel, and Du Pont.

> Served as a member of the Media Plans Board, which reviewed and
> made basic recommendations for all accounts. Acted as consultant
> on business media to many accounts which were basically assigned
> to other buyers. This included both New York and out-of-town
> offices, with some contact with virtually every Estherson
> Associates account.

> Served for four years as a member of the Business Paper Committee
> of the American Association of Advertising Agencies.

1948 - 1951 Print Buyer

> Wrote media recommendations on specific problems and handled
> print buying and estimating for Du Pont, T.W.A., and others.

1945 - 1948 - Production and Traffic Clerk

> Performed normal traffic duties of following preparation of
> material from layout to mailing of plates and insertion dates.

(Continued)

Military Experience: 1942 - 1945, 2nd Lieutenant - U.S. Army Air Force

Education: Haverford College, Haverford, Pennsylvania

Date of Birth: December 1, 1922

Marital Status: Single

References: Available on request.

R. S. WATSON
270 Runnymede Street
Lipton, Arkansas 19701

EMPLOYMENT

1973–1979   Jessica Blaine, Inc. — St. Augustine, Florida

President: activities consisted of planning, account acquisition, creative direction, copy, media selection and related functions.

1972–1973   T. Teaks, Inc. — Reno, Nevada

Account Executive: complete responsibility for all agency activity on Harcourt Brace Jovanovich, Inc., Subaru Automobiles. Assisted as Account Executive on Singer Fabrics and Notions, plus related agency operations, new business and special projects.

1969–1971   Field and Spring International, Inc. — Chicago, Illinois

Assistant Account Executive: Eastern Airlines (Broadcast and Print), functioned under the Y and R training program on the following accounts: Dash, Salvo, Gainesburger, Top Choice, Marshall Cavendish Ltd., Travelers Insurance, Liggett & Myers, General Cigar, Pepsico International, British Rail.

1966–1969   Uni Med, Inc. — Chicago, Illinois

Division Chief: responsible for the supervision and coordination of activities of 27 employees in the Group Contracts Division of the Correspondence Department.

EDUCATION

Hofstra University, Hempstead, L.I., New York
B.S., business administration, 1966.

PERSONAL DATA

Born May 20, 1944. Separated, three children
Height: 5'8", weight: 170 lbs.

REFERENCES

Will be furnished upon request.

Bruce B. Rothschild
718 5th Ave.
N.Y.C., New York 10003
Telephone: (212) 261-5594

Professional Objective

Position in media department. Interested in a media trainee position or a research trainee spot. Have the background and ability to assume immediate responsibilities and progress rapidly.

Education 1973 to 1975

S.I. Newhouse School of Public Communications, Syracuse University, Syracuse, New York 13210
Major Degree: B.S. in Advertising.
Minor: English.
Major Background: Took courses dealing in advertising practices, production, news and copywriting, various media related courses, and communications law.
Activities: Syracuse University Ski Club and Syracuse University Outing Club.
Expenses: Loans, Summer Employment, and University Work-Study jobs (Dorm office clerk, University Union Facility Coordinator).

1971 to 1973

New York Institute of Technology, Old Westbury, New York
Majored in Communications Arts. Special emphasis on Television-Radio production.
Activities: Member of the student senate. Staff member of student radio station WNYT.
Expenses: Loans, summer employment, and weekend employment.

Work Experience September 1975 to May 1978

Fairview Advertising
260 Madison Avenue, New York City, N.Y. 10016
Position: Media Assistant.
Responsibilities: Worked with schedules, contracts; did estimating, planning, space buying, and general problem solving. Did extensive phone contact work with representatives of various media and with clients.
Supervisor: John J. Smith, Media Director.

Personal Data

Born: March 22, 1952. Rockville Center, New York.
Appearance: Height - 6 ft. 1 in., Weight - 170 lbs.
Marital Status: Single.
Residence: Live at parents' home. Can relocate.
Interests: Travel, music, reading, and sports.

Stephanie Andreas   Marital Status: Single
64 London Place   Date of Birth: April 29, 1948
Orange, NJ 07078   Height: 5'3"
(201) 244-9876   Weight: 120 lbs.

Job Objective: To apply my expertise in a medical or hospital lab.

Employment History

    6/73-present   **Medical Technician**

                                             St. John's Hospital, Newark, N.J.
                                           Responsible for all testing in 300-bed
hospital; supervise 4 lab assistants;
responsible for hospital studies of blood,
skin, urine; assist in radioisotope on
thyroid tests; assist in pathological
studies.

    7/70 - 5/73   **Laboratory Assistant**

                                           East Orange General Hospital, East Orange,
N.J. Collected samples and conducted
routine blood tests; conducted prelimi-
nary patient interviews.

Education   B.S., Douglass College, 1970.
                             Chemistry major, biology minor.

Special Interests   Gardening, cooking, playing the piano.

References on request

MERCHANDISER

MARGIE A. THOMPSON
89 WOODRIDGE ROAD
COLUMBUS, OHIO   43212
APARTMENT # 123

(614) 443-7785

EXPERIENCE:
August 1975 -
Present

CERO'S AND KLINES'
Canton, Ohio

Assistant to the Store Manager/Merchandising Hardlines

Redesigned departments including: redefining of classifications, merchandise and fixture presentations resulting
in sales increases of 10-20%.
Coordinated the efforts of buyers and display department
personnel to achieve aesthetically pleasing, cohesive
vignettes representing market trends and store direction.
Created more awareness of merchandise presentation and
coordination throughout the home furnishings divisions.

June 1973-
July 1975

HOUSE FURNISHINGS, INC.

Buyer/Merchandiser/Coordinator: Accessories

Reduced the resource selection by 60% and increased volume
by 15% while opening 50% fewer stores.
Raised the net profitability of department by 35%.
Raised the turnover rate of merchandise in stores from 1.5
to 2.5 times per year via tighter selections, controls and
the implementation of an inventory control system.
Within capacity of merchandising consultant to over 250
stores in the area of gifts and accessories, have shopped
all major national accessory markets and researched, coordinated and published 5 service manuals which are utilized
for resources, merchandise and display techniques.
Directed dealers with designing, merchandising and displaying their in-store gift shops.

January 1970-
June 1973

SUNSHINE DEPARTMENT STORE
224 West Market Street.
Cleveland, Ohio

Department Manager: Men's Accessories, Candy, Smoke Shop

Reduced personnel budget by 30-man-hours per week through
more efficient use of personnel.
Supervised 25 employees.
Reordered all merchandise sold in departments.
Responsible for all department areas including personnel,
housekeeping, displays, merchandising.   (Continued)

EDUCATION: B.S. Business Management
                 Bowling Green University

PERSONAL: Birthdate: 4/7/43
                 Height: 5'7"
                 Weight: 132 lbs.
                 Marital Status: Married

References on Request

METALLURGIST

GEORGE W. WILLIAMS
244 Washington Boulevard
Flushing, New York 11304
212-492-6490

Date of Birth: November 8, 1946
Height: 5'11-1/2"
Weight: 185 lbs.
Marital Status: Married

OBJECTIVE   To obtain position in supervisory capacity with
               Metallurgical Laboratory.

EXPERIENCE

1/75-Date   Technical Advisor and Editor, Scientific Journal of
               America, New York, N.Y. Write and edit articles on
               latest developments and innovations in ferrous
               industries; conduct in-field research for collection
               of data for feature articles; public relations
               responsibilities with domestic industries related
               to metallurgical processes.

5/72-1/75   Production Supervisor, Metallurgical Division,
               CITOR Chemical Laboratories, White Plains, N.Y.
               Conducted quality control checks on Chemical,
               Physical Metallurgy, Metallography regarding future
               production requirements; handled customer complaints
               with respect to both metallurgical and non-metallur-
               gical process deviations; ordered all supplies
               necessary to heat treating; supervised and scheduled
               assignments of laboratory technicians and production
               workers.

8/67-5/70   Metallurgical Trainee, Allison Steel Works,
               Pittsburgh, Pa. Trained in metallurgical aspects
               of metal defect reduction, non-destructive testing,
               chemical analysis development and implementation of
               processes involving physical testing, cost reduc-
               tion; gained experience in Quality Control, including
               statistics control charts, and developed skills in
               both metallurgical and non-metallurgical process
               deviations. Assisted in supervision of eight
               laboratory technicians.

EDUCATION

B.S. in Metallurgical Engineering, June, 1967, Wheeling University,
Pennsylvania.

(Continued)

PROFESSIONAL SOCIETIES

Member of American Society of Mining Engineers, American
Metallurgist Society, Institute of Metallurgical Engineering.

INTERESTS

Skiing, boating, camping, writing for technical journals.

REFERENCES

Furnished on request.

MUTUAL FUND ACCOUNTANT

NIKITA WYCKOFF
2011 Connecticut Road
Island Park, N.Y.   11558
516-889-0448

Born August 2, 1931
5'9", 150 lbs.
Single
Naturalized U.S. Citizen

RESUME CAPSULE: Worked as Mutual Fund Accountant
for twenty years in variety of corporations, also
included thirteen years' experience in bookkeeping.

EXPERIENCE

1973-1979   Mutual Fund Accountant, Capital Advisory Service,
Inc., New York City. Prepared monthly financial
statements; calculated net asset value of Fund's
capital stock; maintained full set of books, including
general ledger; recorded daily transactions and
assigned data for computer processing, calculated
interest on bonds and short-term paper.

1972-1973   Mutual Fund Accountant, Walker's Management, Inc.
New York City. Responsibilities same as above.

1969-1972   Mutual Fund Accountant, J.R. Stern Advisors and
Distributors, New York. Worked on financial statements, general ledger, S.E.C. reports (N-IR and N-IQ),
taxes.

1955-1969   Mutual Fund Accountant and Bookkeeper, Brewster Management
Corporation, Long Island. Complete responsibility for
maintaining Fund's books, including general ledger,
pricing of Fund's shares, supervision of clerical staff
of four, liaison with Custodian and Transfer Agent,
general correspondence and all duties connected with
conducting the Fund's business transactions.

EDUCATION
LL.B. of the University of Riga, Latvia, Faculty of Law and Economics,
1955.

Certificate in Investment Analysis, 1960, Finance Institute of
New York.

LANGUAGES
Fluency in Russian, Latvian, French, German.

INTERESTS
Chess, Backgammon, other table games of skill.

Joanne Mitchell   Born: March 7, 1944
36 Riggs Street   Marital Status: Single
Cedar Rapids, Iowa 52465   Height: 5'7"
(319) 958-9362   Weight: 135 lbs.

Job Objective

Private Nurse

Experience

6/68 - 3/79   Nurse, St. Johns Hospital, Cedar Rapids, Iowa
                   Responsible for general care of patients in
                   cardiac division: took histories, kept charts,
                   administered medication, prepared patients for
                   tests and treatments.

                   Nurse, Cedar Rapids Hospital, Cedar Rapids, Iowa
                   As a staff nurse on surgical floor, duties
                   consisted of preparing patients for operation and
                   treatment, administering medication (kept com-
                   plete records of all narcotics), assisting in
                   physical therapy and attending personal needs of
                   patients.

Education

1962 - 1966   B.S. in Nursing, Iowa State College, Boise, Iowa

Hobbies

          Swimming   Piano
          Sailing   Chess

References

          On request

MARVIN MILTON
24 Woodbine Drive
Cherry Hill, N.J.   08003
(609) 685-4039

PERSONAL

Born October 26, 1938
Married, 3 children
5'10", 185 lbs.

EXPERIENCE

1971-present   Customer Relations Manager, Premium Publishing Company,
                  Morris Hills, N.J. Manage Customer Relations Dept.,
                  with staff of 13 full-time employees. Maintain effective
                  and efficient customer relations, maintain and control
                  procedure of work flow, act as liaison between sales,
                  operations, and customers. Analyze and make decisions
                  for adjustments, credits and debits. Involved in all
                  phases including processing of orders, shipping, returns,
                  sales, credits. Prepare reports (weekly and monthly) on
                  statistics, problems, and make recommendations when needed.
                  Handle all problems related to personnel, vacations, time
                  cards, interviewing, hiring and training.

1965-1971   Administrator-Office Manager, Civic Center, Plainfield,
                  N.J. Maintained and supervised bookkeeping and accounting
                  records according to established practice. A/P, A/R,
                  payroll, purchasing, check reconciliation, general ledger.
                  Prepared periodic financial statements, reviewed budget,
                  maintained accurate membership records; handled enrollment
                  of new members; prepared calendar of events for all
                  affiliated groups, coordinated the use of facilities;
                  supervised building and maintenance staff. Administered
                  and executed all policies made by executive board.

1960-1964   Field Sales Representative, Martin's Gift Shop, Avenue of
                  the Americas, New York. Called on wholesalers, chain and
                  retail stores as representative of manufacturer and
                  importer of novelties, souvenirs, costume jewelry, etc.
                  Involved extensive travel throughout midwest states. Set
                  up and exhibited at numerous trade shows.

(Continued)

MILITARY

1952-1956   U.S. Navy, Honorable Discharge, National Defense and
                 American Theatre Medals, Good Conduct Medal.

EDUCATION

1957-1959   Dearborn Jr. College, Ridgelake, Colorado.
                 Two-year certificate, Business Administration.

1969-1970   Bradley Business School, Rutherford, N.J.
                 Night courses in Business Administration.

INTERESTS

Football, baseball, swimming, reading, active membership in civic
organizations.

OFFSET OPERATOR

Washington J. Brooks
2341 Harrison Avenue
Houston, Texas 77003

(713) 651-9812

Born: January 31, 1940
Divorced / 1 child
5'7" / 148 pounds

Job Objective: **Duplicating Specialist — Photo and Printing**

Experience

1965—1979   Skilled Duplicating Operator
United Oil Company, Houston, Texas

Operated and maintained offset duplicating machines to reproduce black and white or color copies from metal or paper masters. Equipment varied from 1250-multilith, 2650-multilith automatic, to Davidson 400 and 600.

Operated photostat camera to produce prints of varying sizes. Prepared negatives (stripping) for plate-making in black and white and multicolor work. Mixed chemicals needed for photographic process. Prepared black and white slides, ozalids, operated offset camera, and handled some half-tone offset photography.

1962—1965   Duplicating Trainee
Texarco Duplicating Services, Houston, Texas

Acquired a working knowledge of photography, stripping and plate-making Operated automatic feed and manual offset duplicating machines to produce black and white copies from paper masters. Met established standards for producing high quality copies. Made adjustments for proper ink flow, inked machine, adjusted water rollers, set up machine for various types of paper and positioned master as necessary.

Education   Willow Grove High School, Diploma 1957

Military   Served a four-year term in the United States Army.
Honorably Discharged, 1961.

References   On request.

PAYROLL SUPERVISOR

Stanley Y. Gerbreem   Date of Birth: 6-22-49
12 Central Street, South   Single
Omaha, Nebraska 68114   6'1" -- 185 lbs.

(402) 456-0976

Job Goal: Payroll Supervisor

Experience

1971 - present   Vanderbilt, Lowe and Thomas, Inc., Omaha, Nebraska
                 Payroll Clerk
                 _____

                 While in training, became familiar with corporate personnel
                 and payroll policies, various unit payroll practices, benefit
                 plan program, and appropriate tax manuals.

                 Examine and process changes to the basic computerized payroll
                 file for approximately 500 employees. Maintain control totals
                 for different types of changes by unit (increases, new hires,
                 terminations). Examine time sheets and other records to
                 apply overtime and exception pay practices, processing special
                 payments (sales bonus, incentive awards); and prepare manual
                 checks for emergency situations.

                 Maintain employee absence and vacation records. Compose
                 routine correspondence. Solve discrepancy problems.

1969 - 1971   Meyers & Harris Distribution Center, Omaha, Nebraska
                 Clerk in Marketing Research Department
                 _____

                 Performed standardized clerical tasks following company
                 procedures. Maintained salary ledger for department,
                 assembled and classified vouchers, entered postings for
                 the department budgets.

Education   Portland District High School, Portland, Oregon
                  Diploma of Business Studies, 1967

Military   Served a two-year term in the Coast Guard.

References   Available on request.

Personal   Have won two skiing awards and teach skiing weekends.

Barbara Winters
1645 West Brook Drive
Passaic, New Jersey 07056
(201) 455-6767

EMPLOYMENT HISTORY:	WAVERLY CORPORATION (PULP AND PAPER COMPANY), 3722 Boston Post Road, New Rochelle, New York
7/2/73 - Present	Administer Corporate Savings and Investment Plan, Retirement Plan and Long Term Disability Plan.

SAVINGS AND INVESTMENT PLAN

Maintain all records of activity. Review and approve new enrollments and terminations. Calculate and process monthly cash transactions connected with transfer of company and employee funds to the Trustee. Prepare information to Corporate Tax Department in connection with various S.E.C. reports. Assist and advise local Benefits Representatives with administration of the Plan.

RETIREMENT PLAN

Calculate and file with actuaries refunds of contributions on all salaried non-vested terminations. Deposit and refund cash contributions received from foreign and domestic subsidiaries. Act as trouble shooter between hourly locations and actuaries.

DISABILITY PLAN

Calculate monthly Long Term Disability premiums. Coordinate and process salaried Long Term Disability and New York State Disability claims. Maintain all records and correspondence.

11/27/72 - 6/29/73	TRENTON MEMORIAL HOSPITAL, 2167 Arbor Avenue, Trenton, New Jersey (Unemployment Insurance Clerk)

Administered unemployment insurance claims.

(Continued)

4/8/68 -   CLAYTON INDUSTRIES, 6767 Williamsburg Avenue, Trenton, New
  11/22/72   Jersey
                  (Personnel Assistant)

                  Recruited and oriented clerical, production and some technical
                  personnel. Processed merit and cost of living increases.
                  Administered Blue Cross, Major Medical, Life Insurance, Work-
                  men's Compensation, New York State Disability, Unemployment
                  Insurance, etc.

2/14/66 -   WESTBURY INC., 23 West Canal Street, New York, New York
  4/5/68   (Assistant Personnel Supervisor)

                  Recruited, oriented clerical employees. Processed performance
                  appraisals and merit increases. Maintained employee records.

EDUCATION: Villanova University, B.B.A., 1966.

PERSONAL   Date of Birth - 12/25/45, Single. Hobbies - sewing, music.
DATA:

References available on request.

PERSONNEL ADMINISTRATOR

JEANETTE ELWELL   Born February 28, 1932
32-22 224th Street   5' 3", 118 lbs.
Brooklyn, New York   11263   Single
212-962-2668

JOB OBJECTIVE: To apply experience, mature insight, and education
                 to position in personnel administration where
                 effective personnel management can be promoted.

EXPERIENCE PERTINENT TO OBJECTIVE

1959-   Personnel Manager, Hart and Dunlap Co., Inc., New York City.
1979   Reported to Vice President of Personnel in this major publishing
           firm in fulfilling responsibilities as supervisor of personnel
           services for New York office. Conducted salary surveys,
           established salary ranges and progression rates for each level.
           Installed and maintained job evaluation plans, questionnaires,
           application forms, etc. Revised and formulated training programs,
           designed progress reports and initiated appraisal procedures for
           employee performance. Ran successful recruiting campaigns for
           new employees for reference book subsidiary. Initiated and
           implemented programs to improve and utilize potential of staff
           members. Represented company at hearings with City and State
           Boards. Was involved in development of company policies with
           responsibility for interpretation with implementation in every-
           day practice. Consulted with managers on numerous problems such
           as manpower planning, upgrading, performance evaluation.

EDUCATION

M.B.A., Management - Graduate School of Business Administration, New York
University, New York, New York, June 1968.

B.A., History, Rochester University, New York, February 1953.

Personnel Management Course, National Conference Board of Industrial Management,
1963. Techniques and planning for effective personnel programs were developed
with the use of group case histories and lectures.

REFERENCES

Upon request.

BARBARA JO BERNSTEIN
307 East 78th St.
New York, N.Y. 10021
(212) 429-5467

OBJECTIVE

A position in personnel with a salary commensurate with the opportunities afforded.

WORK EXPERIENCE
5/73 to 5/78

Hapcourt Research Company, Inc., 789 Park Avenue, N.Y.C.

Personnel Interviewer

Responsible for all non-exempt and some exempt recruitment for the parent company and several subsidiaries (approximately 1,800 employees).

Counseling duties included employee-subsidiary relations and formal exit interviews.

Involved in special reports dealing with EEO, Affirmative Action programs, Wage and Salary surveys, and employee computerized programs.

Responsible for handling medical and dental benefits for The Psychological Corporation, a subsidiary of 250 employees.

Administrative Assistant

Primary responsibility was to obtain permission to reprint material in our school textbooks; also responsible for some secretarial work.

9/72 to 5/73

E. F. Hutton, 280 Park Avenue, N.Y.C.

Secretary

Responsible for all secretarial duties for an account executive.

(Continued)

EDUCATION   Muhlenberg College, B.A. History, June 1972. Penn State.
                   Instructor's Level I certification in secondary history
                   education. Graduated with a cumulative average of 3.15.

                   Katherine Gibbs, Certificate of Completion ENTREE program,
                   August, 1972.

                   New York University Graduate School of Business
                   Administration, Currently attending evenings, January 1975
                   to present.

PERSONAL DATA   Date of Birth: May 22, 1950   Single   Height: 5'9"
                   Weight: 140 lbs.

Dorothy Rogers
145 Pacific Drive, Apt. 2C
Marine del Ray, CA. 90087
(213) 346-6144

Experience   1970-present
                 Photographer, Wilson Studio, Malibu, CA.
                 Chief photographer in still-life, high
                 fashion studio. Taking pictures, directing
                 models, booking locations...black and white,
                 4 colors.

                 1960-1970
                 Beauty Fashion Photographer. Trend Magazine,
                 New York City, N.Y. Developed analytical
                 themes for feature articles, news stories,
                 and photo essays. Hired and booked models,
                 responsible for stylists.

                 1958-1961
                 Free-lance Photographer

Exhibits   1971
                 Famous Woman, Fine Arts Center, Los Angeles,
                 CA.

                 1966
                 In Black and White, Beveridge Bldg., Chicago,
                 Ill.

Education   Ellison School of Photography, Ellison, Ca.,
                 1960
                 High School of Music and Art, New York City,
                 N.Y., 1958

Personal   Born: 2/18/41
                 Height: 5'9"
                 Weight: 130
                 Marital Status: Divorced

References on request

PHOTOGRAPHER

RESUME OF C. KIMBALL PRETTSON

14 Panther Place
Stamford, Connecticut 06814

Telephone
Days — (203) 674-0867
Eves. — (203) 976-3457

Single   *Born:* October 19, 1949   *Height:* 5' 9"   *Weight:* 135 lbs.

Capabilities:	The ability to work independently and creatively with the maturity necessary to complete high-pressure jobs correctly and on time.
Present Employment:	**Production Manager for Meridian Studios** Port Chester, N.Y. — Meridian is a full service house specializing in large format photography for advertising, slide production, and art work. Meridian services many of the major corporations and agencies in Westchester and Fairfield Counties.
Responsibilities:	• Head up and oversee all in-house production. • Control job flow and client specifics.
Prior Experience: *1973-1976*	**Chief Assistant** to George Taubert, Taubert Studios, Mount Vernon, New York
1971-1973	Owned and ran with partner a commercial studio.
1970-1971	Head of black and white commercial lab.
Professional Education:	Germain School of Photography
Familiar Formats:	Five years extensive 4X5 and 8X10 view plus all small mm. formats.
Job Assignments:	• 4X5 and 8X10 product photography • Catalog Shootings • 2¼ sq. — ad promotion — corporate and college • 4X5 and 35mm. flat art • 35mm. Kodalith slides, negative and positive, hand dyed and jelled • 35mm. Diazo slides • Vu Graphs — Multiple overlays • Mounting and packaging
Darkroom Experience:	Complete black and white capabilities
Background Information:	Born in Greenwich, Connecticut. Educated in public and private schools. Member Indian Harbor Yacht Club. Active sailboat racing skipper. Skiing and paddle tennis

PHYSICAL THERAPIST

Helen Roland
46 Robinwood Drive
Toledo, Ohio 43612

Home phone: 419-236-3715

Employment experience

1967 to present

Mary Magdalene Hospital
45 Parson Street
Toledo, Ohio
Physical Therapist--Children's
Ward. Post-operative and long-term
therapy with preadolescents.
Initiated prosthetic acclimatization
program which was adapted for adults.

1962 to 1967

Perkins University Hospital
Maybury Road
Toledo, Ohio
Part-Time Physical Therapist
This was in conjunction with a degree
program. Worked with geriatric and
juvenile patients.

Education:

1967

Physical Therapist Certification
Perkins University

1962

B.A. Wisconsin University
Major: Biology. Minor: Psychology

Personal:

Born: April 4, 1940.

Marital Status: Married, one child.

Height: 5'3".

Weight: 100 lbs.

REFERENCES ON REQUEST

POLICE OFFICER

Thomas Egan
52 Elm Street
Harrison, New York 10502

Home Telephone: 914-682-4576   Office Telephone: 914-682-1000, ext. 211

WORK EXPERIENCE:

1956-Present   **Harrison Police Force**, Harrison, New York
After four years on force, was promoted to
sergeant in charge of the juvenile division.
In 1968 was promoted to captain and police
chief.

1954-1956   **Patrolman**, New Jersey State Police
Morristown Barracks

EDUCATION:

New Jersey State Police Academy at Morristown, 1954
B.A., Lafayette College, Easton, Pennsylvania, 1948

CLUB MEMBERSHIPS, AFFILIATIONS:

1974-Present: Chairman, Westchester Big Brothers of America
1964-1968:   Secretary Treasurer Patrolman's Benevolent
Association
1960-1968:   Coordination, Police Athletic League

PERSONAL:

Height:	6'1"	Born:	Passaic, New Jersey
Weight	200 lbs.		November 1, 1927
Marital Status:	Married	Children:	Two

REFERENCES: On request

PRODUCTION MANAGER

ELLA TURNER   212-822-9416
4820 Bronx Road
Bronx, New York 10467

EXPERIENCE

July 1973-Present   Production Manager, Publications, Inc., New York City.
                     Serve as liaison between the Editorial and Sales
                     Departments. Responsibilities include the overall
                     preparation and layout of two major trade publications,
                     including annual directories. Design and makeup of ads
                     and reprints, complete follow through of advertising
                     materials, insertion orders and advertisement schedules.
                     Direct contact and working knowledge of printing
                     schedules and full responsibility of and for printing/
                     production costs.

December 1972-   Assistant to the Coordinator, United Society of Magazine
November 1973   Photographers, New York City. Entire processing of ap-
                     plicants and potential members; presenting their work
                     to Board of Trustees for final acceptance to the Society.

July 1971-   Sales Secretary, Media Management, New York City. Handled
November 1972   secretarial duties and expansion into overall partici-
                     pation in circulation and production responsibilities.
                     Varied functions in this position included proofreading,
                     handling of insertion orders, contracts, advertising
                     material and billing.

EDUCATION

Academic Degree from St. Anthony High School - June 1971.

PERSONAL

Date of Birth: February 2, 1953
Single
5'4", 115 lbs.

REFERENCES

Will be furnished upon request.

PROGRAMMER TRAINEE

Maria T. Gonzales
560 Attala Drive
Bakersfield, California 93309

(805) 651-3987

Date of Birth: 4/30/1950
Height: 5'3"
Weight: 111 pounds

Job Objective: Programmer Trainee

Experience

1973-present   Atlas Electronics - Bakersfield, California
                    Computer Operator
                    _____

                    Operates and monitors digital computer equipment
                    (370-155 and 360-65). Follows established programs
                    and new programs under development. Selects
                    appropriate processing devices (card, tape, disc)
                    and loads computer. Observes lights on console and
                    storage devices to report deviations from standards.

                    Maintains records of job performance; checks and main-
                    tains controls on each job. Solves operational
                    problems and checks out new programs; assists in
                    making necessary corrections. Assists less experienced
                    operators.

1972-1973   Bee Newspaper - Modesto, California
                    Bookkeeper/Clerk Typist
                    _____

                    Typed invoices, posted and maintained records and files;
                    made and verified computations. Typed classified ads
                    and sent to composing department.

Education   1972 B.S. degree from University of California
                    Mathematics Major - Business studies and computer training
                    Activities - Advertising Manager of campus newspaper
                               Volunteer hospital work

References   Provided on request.

145

PUBLIC ADMINISTRATOR

FRANK BEATTY
50 Union Boulevard
Union City, N.J.   07087
201-864-4239

Born September 20, 1939
Height: 6' 2-1/2"
Weight: 200 lbs.
Marital Status: Married, no
children

OBJECTIVE: Position with State agency of investigative and
correctional nature on larger scale than that
of previous experience.

EXPERIENCE

1971-Date   <u>Caseworker - Investigator</u>, Union City Dept. of
Social Services. Investigate eligibility and
maintain clients on public welfare.

1966-1971   <u>Parole Officer</u>, Narcotics Division, New Jersey
Narcotic Addiction Control Center. Conducted
investigations, supervised narcotic addicts,
apprehended violators.

EDUCATION

M.B.A., Public Administration, February 1970, Fairleigh
School of Business Administration, Upton University, N.J.

B.B.A., February 1966, Fairleigh School of Business Administration, Upton University, N.J.

HONORS

William Bucknell Scholarship Award
John Fairleigh Scholarship Award
Psi Chi Honorary Professional Psychology Fraternity

INTERESTS

Swimming, tennis, wrestling, bike riding.

REFERENCES

Suitable personal references furnished upon request.

JOANNA CURTIS
29 East 12th Street
New York, New York 10003
212-669-7839

JOB OBJECTIVE   Seeking position as public relations consultant.

EXPERIENCE

1971-present   Legal Secretary, S. Jerome Berg Associates,
                   Bronx, New York. Handle legal correspondence,
                   great deal of technical, legal details requiring
                   knowledge of legal terms and format, much
                   telephone contact with clients, appointment
                   scheduling, often working under pressure to
                   meet court dates, etc. so that necessary
                   documents are completed on time.

1968-1971   French Teacher, Brookville High School, N.Y.

1967-1968   French Translator, Markum Engineering Corp.,
                   New York. Translated correspondence and reports
                   from branch office in Paris. Acted as inter-
                   preter in Public Relations Department and liaison
                   between French engineers and New York office staff.

1965-1967   French Teacher, Strauss High School, New York.

EDUCATION

M.A., 1967, French - Middlebury College, Vermont
B.A., 1965, French - Middlebury College, Vermont

SPECIAL SKILLS

Fluency in French, Spanish, German
Stenotype Machine
Writing and Editing

PERSONAL DATA

Date of Birth: November 9, 1943
Citizenship: U.S.A.
Height: 5' 7"
Weight: 125 lbs.
Marital Status: Single

REFERENCES

Furnished upon request.

CONFIDENTIAL

HELEN C. CHESTERFIELD,   43 Crescent Lane, Port Washington, N.Y. 11050 (516) 384-9227

SUMMARY: Ten years' public relations and advertising experience in multi-division corporation and public relations firms. Direct experience included financial and product publicity; business and technical articles and speeches; institutional and product public relations and advertising; shareholder and employee relations. Supervised department and directed successful efforts of public relations and advertising agencies.

EXPERIENCE: **Director of Communications, GAF, Inc., Woodside, N.Y.**
                  November 1973 to Present — Advertising, public relations, shareholder relations for this American Stock Exchange company.

                  Account Executive, Howard P. Schmidt Associates, New York, N.Y.
                  March 1971 to September 1973 — Corporate, financial and product public relations for industrial, consumer and financial services companies. Corporate planning, executive speeches, annual reports, brochures, feature articles, news releases and scripts. Also analyst meetings, press conferences, marketing seminars, broadcast interviews, corporate advertising. Good relations with all segments of financial community, and trade, general and business media.

                  Account Executive, Spahr, Smith and Associates, New York, N.Y.
                  April 1969 to February 1971 — Supervised corporate and financial public relations activities for client firms (construction, medical products, leisure time, electronics). Wrote and placed news releases, speeches, feature articles, annual reports, brochures and leaflets. Arranged for press conferences, analyst meetings and personal interviews.

                  Advertising and Public Relations Manager, Page Co., Inc., New York, N.Y.
                  May 1960 to March 1969 — Coordinated all internal and external (agency) advertising and public relations activities, scheduled space advertising and product publicity, prepared advertising budgets and analyses. Also originated sales literature, directed mail, organized trade shows, edited sales newsletter and house organ, prepared annual reports and supervised staff of four.

EDUCATION: B.S., New York University (1959)
                  Undergraduate, University of Chicago

PERSONAL: Married, three children, 39 years old

MEMBERSHIP: American Public Relations Society
                  New York Public Relations Association

Gail R. Geltzer
310 West 30th Street
New York, New York 10001
(212) 694-0074

St. Vincent's Hospital - Assistant Director of Public Information
1966-1979

Described, interpreted, promoted and publicized policies, patient care services, medical research, medical, nursing and paraprofessional education programs of this hospital to its various publics to earn their understanding, support and acceptance. (Publics included patients, contributors, staff, faculty and students, trustees, volunteers, other agencies, general and local community.) As editor of an award-winning internal-external house organ, developed ideas, did bulk of writing, total layout and production of five times-a-year, 16,000 circulation publication. Responsibilities included heavy press liaison with science and hospital reporters on daily papers, television and radio stations, news, medical, health and hospital magazines, government press officers, freelance writers, educational film producers. Wrote releases, arranged press conferences. Extensive liaison with public relations officers of affiliated institutions, other health and welfare agencies, city, state and federal health agencies, etc. in joint efforts, exchange of information. Gave public relations' counsel, editorial help to professional staff. Worked with hospital's development office on fund-raising events.

The Salvation Army - Public Information Associate
1960-1966

Planned, wrote, produced major publications interpreting this noted agency's program of family counseling, social action and welfare research to a variety of publics: annual report, a monthly bulletin to contributors, internal staff house organ, bimonthly newsletter for board and committee members, fund-raising campaign literature, brochures. Wrote radio and television spots, speeches as needed. Wrote and/or placed news and feature stories ranging from pilot demonstration study results to appraisals of legislation in fields of health, housing, aging, family and child welfare, narcotics addiction, courts, etc. Wrote case stories for Times Neediest Cases, of which agency was a major beneficiary. Job required keeping abreast of entire social welfare field and being able to translate into lay language,technical, often complicated concepts of caseworks, medicine, psychiatry, community organization and legalities.

(Continued)

The American Nursing Association - Publications and Public Relations Consultant
1957-1960

Disseminated information about ANA's Department of Hospital Nursing to membership, allied professional groups (American Health Care Association, etc.)
and public through articles, books, brochures, press releases and promotional
materials. Planned, wrote, produced pamphlets, newsletters, including national
newsletter for psychiatric aids and technicians funded by a pharmaceutical
company.

American Paramedical Association - Director of Public Information
1956-1957

Directed recruitment program for occupational therapists under grant from
National Foundation. Created recruitment literature, supervised distribution
nationally to prospective students, universities, guidance counselors, hospital
and medical groups assisting with recruitment. Worked with newspapers, magazines, radio, television nationally. Traveled extensively to spur recruitment
activities on state and local level; extensive liaison work with federal
agencies.

Bridgeport University - Public Relations, School of Nursing
1955-1956

As branch office of Bridgeport Information Bureau, planned and directed student recruitment program. Wrote, placed news and feature stories; produced
recruitment literature; established contacts with prospective students,
faculty, guidance personnel, alumnae. Responsible for fund-raising activities for an endowed university chair in nursing.

New York's Children Hospital - Assistant to Director of Public Relations
1949-1953

Presented stories of services, achievements, needs of hospital, working with
newspapers, magazines, radio, television, educational films. Wrote, produced
bimonthly staff house organ and semiannual magazine for contributors.
Developed and wrote handbooks, pamphlets for patients, staff, donors, nursing
school applicants and nursing staff. Assisted staff in preparing manuscripts
for professional publications. Helped plan special events, tours.

Other experience

Three years, general news and feature writing, The Chappaqua Herald, one of
Westchester's largest daily papers.

(Continued)

Gail R. Geltzer   -3-

Professional Memberships

American Association of Writers, East Coast Chapter; New York Public Relations
Association.

Education

B.A., Journalism, Queens College
M.A., Political Science, Cornell University

Personal

Born: December 4, 1922
Height: 5'3"
Weight: 120 lbs.
Marital Status: Single

Note: *A 3-page résumé such as this is very rare. It is to be used only in exceptional circumstances and even then can work to the detriment of the job seeker.*

HOWARD K. DONALDSON
1170 East Sycamore Lane
Nashville, Tennessee 37204
(615) LO-3-5341

EXPERIENCE:

11/75–Present:

NBC News Election Unit, 30 Tyson Plaza, Atlanta, Georgia.

Work on a free-lance basis assisting in the process of public opinion polling. Wrote reports for management on the administration of the polling operation.

Prior to 1975:

M & M Pharmacy, 191 Spruce Street, Atlanta, Georgia.

Worked in all phases of neighborhood retail pharmacy except professional services for a period of nine years on both a part-time basis during the school year and full-time basis during the summer.

Summer 1974:

Volunteer work at the South Side Legislative Service Center for Assemblyman Tyson. Duties included handling constituent problems, with heavy emphasis on writing correspondence and knowledge of city and state agency functions.

EDUCATION:

2/73–1/75

Richmond College, Richmond, Virginia.

Awarded B.A. in Political Science with Honors in January 1975.

In 1974, participated in Georgia State Assembly Internship Program as a legislative research assistant in the office of then Deputy Minority Leader John Tyson.

Participated in Atlanta Government Internship Program working in the office of Councilman Thomas Sample.

9/70–6/72

University of Georgia, Atlanta, Georgia.

9/66–6/70

Sainthood Preparatory High School, 1150 Carroll Street, Atlanta, Georgia.
Academic Diploma

PERSONAL BACKGROUND:

Born March 25, 1952
5'9", 140 lbs.
Single
Ability to speak, write and read French.
Interested in politics, movies, tennis, reading and writing.

References will be furnished upon request.

RESEARCHER/RECENT COLLEGE GRADUATE

Joan Jumont
220-B\South Beron Street
Byron, Pa. 16917

(814) 909-3516

EXPERIENCE:
1975-present

Penn State Sports Information. State College, Pa.
Responsible for writing releases on individual women
athletes; produce game programs and press guides for
women's teams, gathering and organizing team histories
and statistics; serve as personal liaison between teams
and media; active by phone and mail in contacting opponents
for their records and statistics.

1975

WRSC Radio. State College, Pa.
Gathered, wrote and produced news; responsible for writing
and producing shows on State College athletes and coaches,
both men and women; organized and developed community-
oriented program on "Women's Equality Day"; responsible for
researching and writing various radio spots; Bicentennial
Minutes and Sports Quiz questions.

1973-1975

Pennsylvania Mirror. State College, Pa.
Women's sports' feature writer; also sent letter-series
from abroad.

1973-1975

Stringer for several newspapers.

PUBLICATIONS:

Sportswoman - January-February, 1975.
womenSports - February, 1976.

EDUCATION:

Pennsylvania State University, B.A. June, 1975

Major: English -- Writing Option
Minor: Journalism and Philosophy

Participated in such extracurricular activities as sports-
writing for school paper. Played three varsity sports for
four years. Part-time jobs and an athletic scholarship
helped finance college expenses. All-American.

Worked as an intern in Sports Information Department of
Penn State.

(Continued)

PERSONAL
INFORMATION: Single, age 23. Born, April 12, 1953.
                    Toured with United States' Women's Lacrosse Touring Team,
                    1975. Coach and play lacrosse. Volunteer as publicity
                    chairperson for Mideast Field Hockey Association; also
                    serve as vice-president. Have spoken publicly on problems
                    of women's sports information and on international lacrosse.
                    Have studied and traveled extensively in Europe.

REFERENCES: Personal references on request.

RESTAURANT MANAGER

Paul R. Joseph
2803 Chesapeake St., NW
Washington, D.C. 20008
(202) 345-9876

Employment Objective

To manage dinner-trade continental restaurant in a suburban
setting.

Employment Record

1973-present
Green Door Restaurant, Silver Springs, Md.
Assistant Manager to owner-manager. Supervise
kitchen, dining and bar staff of 35. Approve
menus, maintain food and linen stocks. Initiated wine listing and cellar.

1969-1973
Eight O'Clock Cafes, Washington, D.C., Virginia
and Maryland. Assistant Quality Control Director
for cafe chain. Assessed and maintained performance
standards at seven (originally three) breakfast
cafes: food, service, etc. Prepared reports and
made recommendations for improvements.

1966-1968
Red Clock Luncheonette, Baltimore, Md.
Lunchtime Manager. Supervised lunchtime
trade at busy neighborhood-type restaurant;
filled in as cook, as needed. Maintained
receipts.

1962-1966
Rose's Inn, Elkton, Md. Cook. Prepared American/
Continental meals in small, family-type restaurant.

Education

Completed two years at University of Maryland, Accounting major.
Northeast High School, Baltimore, Md.--Academic Diploma, 1962.

Born: December 1944
Married, two children
Height: 5'11"
Weight: 190 lbs.

RESTAURANT MANAGER

Cheryl Newman   Born: May 8, 1947
1231 Orchid Street   Height: 5 ft., 7 in.
Los Angeles, California   90068   Weight: 125 lbs.
Phone: (213) 989-2406   Married, no children

JOB OBJECTIVE

Management of American/Continental restaurant in Greater Los Angeles area.

EXPERIENCE

June 1970 -   The French Chef
Present   12 Los Angeles Boulevard, Los Angeles, California

Assistant Manager — General food service and managerial assistance in this
eighty table restaurant. Oversee luncheon and dinner kitchen and dining
staffs. Maintain wine and food stocks. Have developed novel seasonal menus
in consultation with chef, which have significantly increased volume of
business.

September 1968 -   The Oasis Hotel
May 1970   15 Main Street, Dallas, Texas

Assistant Banquet Manager — Responsibility for planning and coordination of
100 banquets and private parties per year for from 10-500 guests (business
meetings, personal celebrations, community events). Meal planning and "theme"
development in consultation with banquet hosts.

June 1966 -
September 1968

Waitress and **Cashier** at the Oasis Hotel, in both luncheonette and formal dining
room.

EDUCATION

1971 Successful completion of Restaurant Management course, offered by
      Restaurant Associates of the United States, Inc., Los Angeles, California

1967 A.S. in Food Services, Dallas Junior College, Dallas, Texas

1965 Commercial diploma, Dallas Vocational High School, Dallas, Texas

OTHER ACTIVITIES

Vice Chairman, Los Angeles Restaurant Council

Chairman, Committee for Neighborhood Development, Los Angeles Chamber of
Commerce

REFERENCES

Available upon request

156

SALES ENGINEER

Jeremy Gibbons   Date of Birth: 7/7/45
186 Intracostal Highway   Weight: 185 lbs.
Boca Raton, Florida 33448   Height: 5'11"
(305) 965-9328   Married - 3 Children

Ten years' professional experience in engineering salesmanship.

> OBJECTIVE: To serve initially in sales engineering
>   capacity (sophisticated mechanical equipment)
>   and ultimately enhance responsibilities
>   toward engineering management.

EXPERIENCE

Senior Consultant

The Southern Sun Inc., Boca Raton, Florida - 1974 to date
This position involves the professional selection and sales
of real estate investments, requiring knowledge of tax laws
and shelters as well as applicable real estate laws and
geographical growth trends.

Sales Engineer

Hobart Air Compressor Corporation, Highland Beach, Florida -
1970/1974
This position required the sales of industrial air compressors
and their intrinsic components. These components included
regulating, drive, and air drying systems and their auxiliary
support accessories. As technical salesman, incorporated
the attributes of an applicable engineer, sales representative and a field service engineer. A successful sale required the paralleling of stipulated specifications with the
most reliable, effective and economical systems. Frequently
assisted with engineering, assembling, and authoring of
facility expansion or new plant construction specifications.
Often, the installation of new equipment demanded the coordination, instruction, and supervision of mechanical and electrical contractors. Subsequent start-up and troubleshooting
required the establishment of a working relationship with
plant and maintenance personnel.

Student Trainee

Miami Naval Laboratories, Miami, Florida - 1965/1970
In conjunction with five year cooperative program, participated in developing, assembling, plotting, and recording
data while working with engineers in the research and
development of shipboard fire fighting systems, high strength
steels and titanium for submarine hulls, and damping materials
for sonar dome application.

(Continued)

157

EDUCATION

Miami University, Miami, Florida - Mechanical Engineering
B.M.E. June 1970 (Dean's List).

AFFILIATIONS and
LICENSES

Associate Member - American Society of Mechanical Engineers,
F.A.A. Airframe Mechanics License, Florida Teaching
Credential, Florida Real Estate Association.

PERSONAL

Sportsminded (played baseball and
basketball in college), willing
to travel and relocate

References furnished upon request.

CLAUDIA MORESCO
80 Central Park West
New York, New York 10014

Date of Birth: October 1, 1946
Single, no dependents
5'8", 130 lbs.

212-349-1138

RÉSUMÉ CAPSULE   Major career achievements and satisfactions have
come from positions with responsibility for the
identification and resolution of problems. Skilled
in decision-making, including the organization
and analysis of data, evaluation of alternative
solutions, selection of the optimal approach,
and negotiation for the implementation of the
decision. Experience in both line and staff
positions and strong interpersonal skills.
Results-oriented, learn quickly, and enjoy
challenge. Accomplishments in all positions are
substantiated by rapid salary growth.

EXPERIENCE

July, 1972-
Present

**Manager, Academic Market Development, Book and
Information Services**, Walton and Champion Companies,
Walton, New York. Sales analysis and strategic
planning for existing academic market (college and
university libraries). New product development
including market research, evaluation of external
new ventures proposals, initiation of new products
and services, financial analyses, and design of
marketing offer. Exploration and recommendation
of new market segmentation, development of marketing
strategies for these segments, preparation of
financial projections, and implementation of accepted
proposals.

June, 1969-
June, 1972

Gift and Exchange Librarian, Barnard Libraries,
Rochester, New York. Establishment of a department
to administer the acceptance and review of gifts
to the University libraries. Preparation of a
uniform gift policy and procedure manual for ten
campus libraries. Negotiation and administration
of the exchange of materials with foreign libraries,
particularly in the Soviet Union and Latin America.
Negotiation with dealers for the sale of unneeded
material. Supervision of ten employees.

(Continued)

EDUCATION

M.S.L.S., DeWitt University, January 1971.
M.A.T., Manchester University, June 1967 - Majors: History and Education.

HONORS

Dean's List all semesters
Phi Beta Kappa
Beta Phi Mu honorary

INTERESTS

American architectural history and historic preservation; creative
photography.

```
June Brown                              Born:   May 10, 1949
30 Broad Street                         Status: Married
Atlanta, Georgia    30397               Height: 4'11"
(404) 821-5994                          Weight: 100 lbs.
```

Job Objective: A responsible and challenging opportunity
                    in the administrative area of sales.

Experience:
1971-present   National Accounts Manager, Beautiful
                    Hair and Cosmetics, Inc., Atlanta,
                    Georgia
                    Responsible for a $6 million sales volume
                    in territory east of Mississippi includ-
                    ing hiring and training all new sales
                    personnel, supervising and coordinating
                    activities of all Manufacturers' Repre-
                    sentatives; have increased sale volume
                    30% since April 1976.

Education:
1967-1971   B.A. - University of Georgia

References: Appropriate references will be submitted
                    upon request.

SALESPERSON

Edward Salson
144-30 Ford Brooks Road
Citadel, California 95610

Telephone: (916) 539-8486
Status: Married
Age: 34
Born: October 19, 1942

**business
experience**

October 1975 —
March 1979

Gibson Color Systems, Hudson, New Hampshire

Offset preparatory firm located in New Hampshire with a New York Sales Office.

Salesperson — Developing and servicing accounts handled out of the New York area. Estimated cost of preparatory work including separating and stripping job into position. Handling color correcting press proofs and detail work pertaining to a given job.

December 1968 —
September 1975

Shank Graphics, Chicago, Illinois

Litho and Gravure separator with a St. Paul Office.

Sales and Sales Service — Responsibilities included servicing established accounts and opening up new accounts. Did all the estimating for the St. Paul office.

February 1966 —
December 1968

Baronet Litho Company, Jamestown, Virginia

Small commercial printer. Equipment included a 60-inch four-color press. Plant had complete facilities including stripping, platemaking and bindery and mailing department.

Assistant to Plant Manager — Handled all jobs received from salespeople. Made out job tickets and job layouts. Followed through on all jobs in various stages of production. Ordered paper and other items necessary to produce final product.

education

Rochester Institute of Technology

Earned A.A.S. degree in Photographic Science, 1962
Earned B.S. in General Printing, 1966

references

Will be furnished upon request.

SALES PROMOTER

GREGG D. LEWIS
1085 WARBURTON AVENUE, APARTMENT 808
YONKERS, NEW YORK 10701
914/423-5858

EXPERIENCE

MILLER PRODUCTS, DIVISION OF   MAY 1974 to PRESENT
MILLER-WALLER, INC.

Sales Promotion Manager

> Coordinate promotions for brand and sales management.
> Includes: budgeting, planning, creative and complete
> implementations of plans.

> Manage department of four. Responsibilities for all
> sales promotional materials: artwork, printing, displays,
> premiums, sampling and couponing.

> Negotiate for services of mailing and sampling executions,
> fulfillment houses, and coupon clearing organizations.

> Successfully introduced Dri XX Spray, Dri XX Roll On
> Deodorant and Dew Drops with Fluoride: developed and
> executed promotion plan and strategy.

> Promotion budget of $10,000,000.

BEAUTIFUL HAIR, INC.   FEBRUARY 1972 to MAY 1974

Product Promotion Manager

> Responsible for all retail promotion programs in the Hair
> Color and Toiletries Division: trade promotions, collateral
> material, pricing, sales objectives and advertising plans
> by sales region.

> Developed promotion plans and executed them for new products:
> trade strategy, sampling, couponing, ad sales materials.
> New products include Essence Shampoo that grew to number
> three in shampoo market.

> Worked closely with research, production planning, legal,
> graphic suppliers and ad agency.

> Promotion budget of $12,000,000.

> Heavy business travel.

(Continued)

163

Assistant Product Promotion Manager

Assisted the position "Production Promotion Manager" in all areas
explained.

Sales Representative   JANUARY 1968 to FEBRUARY 1972

   Managed merchandise shows for company in local markets.
   Responsibility for sales volume in 150 direct and indirect
   accounts. Worked closely with company research in new
   product tests including: implementation of new product
   sales plans, weekly audits and test analysis.

EDUCATION

   University of North Carolina, 1963-1967
   B.S. in Business Administration/Marketing

PERSONAL

   February 5, 1944
   Married, One Child
   5'11", 160 lbs.

SENIOR COUNSELOR

Khanh Van Chen
488-1/2 State Street
San Francisco, California 94063
(415) 555-2345

Born: 1/24/47
Marital Status: Single
Weight: 155 lbs.
Height: 5'7"

Five years' professional and educational experience in counseling.

OBJECTIVE: To augment professional placement service by contributing expertise in interviewing, personnel, and guidance counseling.

AMPLIFICATION: To serve organization in private industry and ultimately develop skills for managerial position.

EXPERIENCE

Program
Coordinator

San Francisco Manpower Corporation, San Francisco, California - 1974 to date
This position involves the coordination of six dissimilar office skill training programs encompassing paraprofessional and professional personnel. As program coordinator and senior counselor, supervise thirty-four staff members and one hundred thirty trainees for each rotating cycle. Frequently instrumental in placing graduating trainees to applicable jobs and training them accordingly. Utilize public relations skills during heavy telephone work in contacting and solidifying prospective employers.

Publishing
Secretary

Santana Publishing Company, San Francisco, California - 1/73 to 4/74
This position required the screening and interpreting of telephone calls, written and oral communications concerning inter-office memorandums, and correspondences between management and accounting staff personnel.

Graduate
Assistant

University of Nebraska, Smokeville, Nebraska - 9/72 to 12/73
In conjunction with work-study tuition program, arranged class schedules for students. Counseled foreign students with their academic, social, language adjustment, family, and immigration problems by applying principles of guidance.

EDUCATION

University of Nebraska, Smokeville, Nebraska - M.Ed., 1973
Major: Guidance and Counseling

University of Taiwan, Taiwan - B.A., 1972
Major: English

(Continued)

165

SPECIAL AWARDS

Scholarship to attend world-wide guidance and counseling
convention. Coordinator of foreign students workshop.
Champion debator, third year, college.

PUBLICATIONS

Editor - newsletter and brochure for San Francisco Manpower
Corporation.

REFERENCES

Available upon request.

Dorothy Turner
415 Oakes Street
St. Paul, Minnesota   55149
(612) 654-1234

Experience

April 1975 -
present

Medical Caseworker, Catholic Churches, St. Paul,
Minnesota. Interview patients and their families
at St. Claire's Hospital to ascertain needs of
home care; arrange for volunteer nursing and
housekeeping and child care assistance.

July 1965 -
March 1975

Family Caseworker, K.H. Psychiatric Clinic,
St. Paul, Minnesota. Conducted therapy sessions
for teenagers, adults and children; interviewed
families of patients to determine financial
competency and arranged for financial help.

Education

1965

M.S.W. - Columbia School of Social Work,
         New York City

1964

B.A. - University of Minnesota, St. Paul,
       Minnesota

Personal

Date of Birth: November 4, 1942
Height/Weight: 5'1"/103 lbs.
Marital Status: Single

References

Available upon request.

SOCIAL WORKER

Adrienne Smithfield
22 Olive Tree Street
Kansas City, Missouri 64116

(816) 546-9865

Date of Birth: January 14, 1946

Place of Birth: Brooklyn, New York

Height and Weight: 5'6" — 120 lbs.

Marital Status: Single

EXPERIENCE

1970–present   **Children's Caseworker,** Angel of Mercy Home. Kansas City, Mo. Interview children and families of children at Angel of Mercy Home. The home takes both orphans and children from inadequate homes. Do full investigations. Follow up. Make recommendations concerning children.

1968–1970   **Family Caseworker,** Kansas City State Hospital. Interviewed members of families at the hospital or at their homes. Helped to make for better adjustment. Proposed plans for assisting patients.

EDUCATION

B.S., Social Work, Southern Missouri State College, Springfield, Missouri. Concentrated training in social work with an emphasis on psychiatric and pediatric.

PROFESSIONAL AFFILIATIONS

National Association of Social Workers and National Caseworkers Ass'n.

INTERESTS

Have traveled all over the world. Hobby is travel, and travel on vacation every year. Speak Portuguese fluently.

REFERENCES

References covering all phases of education and experience on request.

SUPERVISOR (INDUSTRIAL)

CLYDE HENLEY
P.O. Box 92
Cranberry Lake, N.J. 08540
609-346-1130

PERSONAL

Born June 27, 1934
5' 10", 180 lbs.
Married, no children

RESUME CAPSULE: Twenty years' experience as Industrial Foreman,
with superior mechanical ability, production
efficiency, leadership and excellent record in
labor relations.

EXPERIENCE

1958-present   Foreman, Ginger Beverages Company, Marshall,
New Hampshire. One of the largest manufacturers of ginger beverages and crystallized
ginger products in the United States. Supervise work of eighteen employees operating
ginger presses, pulverizers, and separators,
producing four varieties of ginger flavored
beverages and confections. Full responsibility
of hiring and supervising employees, training
operators, and establishing work hours and
shifts. Excellent rapport with employees
resulting in minimal grievances with union.

1956-1958   Foreman, Spartan Separators, Inc., Madison,
N.J. One of America's major manufacturers
of separating equipment for use in food processing. Worked in machine assembly department
as night supervisor with full responsibility
for faultless assembly of food processing
equipment.

1952-1956   Tool and Die Maker, Waterford Machine Production Company. Suggested design modifications,
kept production moving. Worked as assistant
night superintendent during rush periods.

(Continued)

EDUCATION

Graduate Brooklawn High School, Brooklawn, N.J. - 1952.
(Mechanical)

REFERENCES

Upon request.

SUPERVISOR (ANY FIELD)

William Fredericks
314 San Fernando Avenue
Hohokus, New Jersey 07423   Telephone: (201) 456-4921

Job Objective: To obtain a position in a field where past supervisory
                experience may eventually be utilized.

Past Experience

May 1975 to Present: Winkler, Cantor and Pomboy (Investments),
                            N.Y., N.Y. (Experience similar to that stated
                            for D.H. Blair and Co.)

February 1968 to   As Supervisor, responsible for entire work output
August 1974   and efficiency of Order Room; proper execution
D.H. Blair and Co.   of orders for brokers, banks and institutional
(Investments) N.Y., N.Y.   funds; assisted brokers in general operations;
                            served as liaison with other brokerage firms on
                            daily transactions and problems. Position required
                            knowledge of stock exchange operations, figure
                            aptitude, decision-making and absolute accuracy
                            under extreme pressure.

1962 to 1968:   Senior Order Clerk and supervisor of branch
                            office of Tessel, Paturick and Ostrau, Inc.
                            (Investments) N.Y., N.Y.

1950 to 1962:   Cashier with Merrill, Lynch, Pierce, Fenner and
                            Smith, N.Y., N.Y. - handled large volumes of cash
                            and securities; was bonded; supervised three
                            cashier clerks; trained approximately 25 broker
                            trainees in all phases of backstage branch opera-
                            tions.

Education: Special Schools: Finance Institutes for
                                              special courses in connec-
                                              tion with banking and
                                              brokerage operations--1950.

                            High School Graduate -- 1948.

Personal: Date of Birth: December 26, 1930.
                            Married. Two children.

171

Marilyn Conklin Rogers
57 Lee Avenue
Columbus, Ohio 42317
Home phone: (614) 456-2397
Business phone (614) 675-9000

Experience

1967 to present   Receptionist/Switchboard Operator

Pathway Employment Agency, Columbus, Ohio.
Responsibilities include operating busy 555
board, greeting job applicants and clients,
administering and grading typing tests,
filing and assisting in mailings.

1952 to 1967   Receptionist

Regal Paper Company, Columbus, Ohio.
Handled busy monitor board, and all
bookkeeping including accounts
receivable.

Education

Commerce High School, Columbus, Ohio.
Commercial Diploma. Graduated June, 1952.

Personal

Date of birth: July 3, 1934

Height: 5' 4"

Weight: 110 lbs.

Marital Status: Married, no children

References on request.

SYSTEMS ANALYST

Kevin J. Hutchins
69 Marrietta Drive
Dallas, Texas 75234

Born: May 16, 1950
Height: 5'11"
Weight: 151 lbs.
Single

Telephone: (214) 459-9345

Job Objective: Systems Analyst

Experience

1974-1979 Programmer Supervisor
           Hartman Oil Company   Dallas, Texas

           Writes computer programs, developing block diagrams,
           utilizing available software and operating systems, and
           coding machine instructions. Originates block diagrams,
           working from outlines of proposed systems, develops file
           sizes, programming specifications. Determines appropriate
           use of tape or disk files, printer, etc. Selects in-house
           software or sub-routines to run in connection with program.

           Writes machine instructions, tests, debugs, and assembles
           program. Documents overall system and develops data control
           procedures. Advises and instructs less experienced pro-
           grammers and prepares operating instructions.

1970-1974 Programmer
           Live Oak Electronics   Houston, Texas

           As a trainee for six months, became proficient in COBOL
           programming. Coded well-defined systems logic flow charts
           into computer machine instructions using COBOL. Coded sub-
           routines following specifications, file size parameters,
           block diagrams. Performed maintenance tasks and patching
           to established, straightforward programs. Documented all
           programs as completed. Tested, debugged and assembled programs.

Education

           Levitt High School, Temple, Texas - Graduated 1968.

           Houston Community College - 1968-1970. Completed two-year course.

References

           Provided on request.

TEACHER (ELEMENTARY)

ROSETTA BROWN
55 Atlanta Avenue
Roselle, New York   14512

716-366-9032

Date of Birth: August 4, 1933
Married, no dependents
5' 6", 135 lbs.

EXPERIENCE

9/62-6/78   Elementary Teacher, Greendale Public Schools, Greendale, New
            York. Taught fourth and fifth grades. Complete responsibility
            for the writing, reading and research for a Teacher's Kit -
            Children's Literature. (A synopsis, discussion questions and
            enrichment multi-media activities for over 55 outstanding
            children's novels.)

9/56-6/62   Elementary Teacher, Greendale Public Schools, Greendale, New
            York. Taught second and third grades. Participated in much
            curriculum work, area of upgraded classes and inter-age
            grouping.

2/55-6/56   Receptionist, Robinson and Sons, New York City.

10/54-1/55 Saleswoman, The Tog Shop, New York City.

7/53-6/54   Reservationist, Landover Air Lines, New York, N.Y.

EDUCATION

M.A., June 1959 - Adelphi University. Elementary Education.

Permanent Certification, 1958.
Common Branch Subjects (1-6).
The University of the State of New York.

B.A., June 1953 - Russell College. English Major.

INTERESTS

Ballet, theatre, reading, writing juvenile poetry and short stories.

REFERENCES

Will be furnished upon request.

ALYSON REXDALE
60 West End Avenue
New York, N.Y. 10023

(212) 866-5332

Personal Data

Date of Birth: May 20, 1950
5' 9", 135 lbs.
Single

EXPERIENCE:

1975–1979   Teacher, Stuyvesant Elementary School, Rochester, New York. Took into account long-range goals of individual students as well as class as a unit, and developed and organized unit in consumer education utilizing visual and audio media. Created and developed working models for use of children to promote coordination and mental stimulation.

1971–1972   Tutored German children in English while at German University in Stuttgart on Exchange Study Program, 1971-72.

EDUCATION:

M.S., Elementary Education, Brampton College, Rochester, N.Y. 1975.

New York State Teacher's Certificate (N-6) #489664101, effective September, 1975.

B.A., Psychology. State University of New York at Albany, 1973.

SPECIAL RECOGNITION:

New York State Regents Scholarship — 1969-73.

REFERENCES:

Will be furnished upon request.

TEACHER / INSTRUCTOR

Robert R. Abbey
48 Mingus Circle
Bayonne, New Jersey 07002

PERSONAL

Born: April 23, 1949
Married - No Children
Height - 5' 10"
Weight - 160

OBJECTIVE: Appointment on teaching staff of small private
              institution in rural area, preferably in
              New York State.

EXPERIENCE:

April 1974-   Teacher/Instructor in Charge of Training and
Present   Development, Eastern Academy, Fort Lee,
                  New Jersey.

September 1973-   Assistant Dean of Students, Parkwood Junior
March 1974   College, Parkwood, New Hampshire. In charge
                  of all student personnel programs, including
                  Career Counseling, Job Placement, Student
                  Government, Admissions Recruitment, Discipline,
                  Athletics, Cultural Development, and Student
                  Welfare Benefits.

September 1971-   Instructor, Glendale High School, Glendale,
June 1973   N.Y. Taught basic Art Courses and American
                  History.

EDUCATIONAL
BACKGROUND

B.S. Education (History), 1970 - St. Michael's College,
New Jersey.

M.A. (History/English), 1971 - Wayne University, Michigan.

REFERENCES will be furnished upon request.

WAGE AND SALARY SUPERVISOR

Lindsay Marie Wells
3546 Swarr Run Road
Lancaster, Pennsylvania 17603
(717) 955-2937

<u>Personal Data:</u> Birthdate: 5/4/47
Marital Status: Single

EXPERIENCE:

May 1972-
present

NATIONAL INSTITUTE OF CERTIFIED PUBLIC ACCOUNTANTS
Manager, Salary Administration - Responsible for administration of salary increase program including promotional
increases, adjustments, monthly merit increase reviews,
performance appraisal program and job evaluation. Conducting compensation surveys to determine necessity of adjusting
exempt and non-exempt salary ranges. Participating in
various compensation surveys. Maintaining employee budget.
Developing and revising policies and procedures. Counseling
employees. Advising personnel employees on job-related
problems. Administration and supervision of personnel
department in Director's absence.

January 1971-
May 1972

BOOKER AND BOOKER
Personnel Assistant - Responsible for smooth running of
personnel; function on a day-to-day basis included interviewing and hiring of administrative staff, obtaining
temporary personnel, supervising work-study employees,
and keeping personnel records. Prepared and filed various
governmental reports including Veteran Reports. Processed
some benefits claims and administered the salary increase
program.

June 1969-
December 1967

WATERMAN HOUSE, INC.
Wage and Salary Specialist - Responsible for maintaining an
equitable salary administration program, including meeting
with department managers in order to study and analyze jobs,
preparation of job descriptions, evaluation of jobs using
established system to determine grades and prepare records
of validity. Developed new evaluation system for exempt
and non-exempt employees, Prepared and maintained merit
increase budget and rate schedules, and organization charts
and listings for all divisions.

EDUCATION:

1965-1967   Pitt Community College - A.A. Degree (Psychology).

1971-1974   Various AMA and Commerce and Industry Courses dealing with
                Personnel.

(Continued)

ACTIVITIES:

February 1970 -   Member of the New York City Jaycees, an international
present   community service and leadership training organization.

                     References available upon request.

Résumé Work Sheets

Now you are ready to get started in the actual writing of your unique résumé. The following work sheets will help you to include all the necessary information and arrange it in a concise organized manner.

After you have completely filled out the pertinent sections on pages 180 to 202, you will have gathered all of the essential material for your résumé and will be ready to arrange it in whichever format you have selected.

Fill out the following work sheets *carefully*. Be sure all information is correct (re-check your dates), because this information will become the heart and soul of your final résumé, which may be drafted on pages 210 to 214.

FOR EXPERIENCED WORKER WITHOUT COLLEGE

I. Identifying Information:

Name: _____
If married woman, include married and maiden names.

Address: _____
Street and number, city, state, and zip code.

Home Phone: _____
Be sure to give area code.

Business Phone: _____
Be sure to give area code.

If business phone should be confidential, so state, i.e., Business phone: (212) 555-1280 (confidential).

II. Job Objective:

Remember, the job objective is optional, but if used, it must be brief. The only time a job objective MUST be used is if you are changing fields.

_____

_____

_____

_____

III. Résumé Capsule:

The résumé capsule, like the job objective, may be left out unless you are trying to change fields.

_____

_____

_____

_____

_____

IV. Employment History:

Your employment history should be listed in inverse chronological order.

Name of Company: _____

Address of Company: _____

_____

_____

Job Title: _____

Dates:	Description of Responsibilities:
From *To*	
(mo./yr.) *(mo./yr.)*	

_____   _____

_____

_____

_____

_____

_____

_____

_____

Name of Company: _____

Address of Company: _____

_____

_____

Job Title: _____

Dates: Description of Responsibilities:

From   *To*
(mo./yr.)   *(mo./yr.)*

_____   _____

_____

_____

_____

_____

Name of Company: _____

Address of Company: _____

_____

_____

Job Title: _____

Dates: Description of Responsibilities:

From   *To*
(mo./yr.)   *(mo./yr.)*

_____   _____

_____

_____

_____

_____

_____

_____

Name of Company: _____

Address of Company: _____

_____

_____

Job Title: _____

Dates: Description of Responsibilities:

From   *To*
(mo./yr.)   *(mo./yr.)*

_____   _____

_____

_____

_____

_____

_____

V. Educational History:

List information about your high school.

Dates: Name of High School:
From   *To*
(year)   *(year)*

_____   _____

Address of High School:

_____

Diploma Earned:

_____

_____

_____

Honors: _____

_____

Special Activities
Worth Mentioning: _____

_____

_____

VI. Personal Information:

Height: _____ Willing to Relocate: _____

Weight: _____ Willing to Travel: _____

Date of Birth: _____ Hobbies or Interests: _____

Marital Status: _____ _____

Military Service (optional):

From   *To*
(mo./yr.) *(mo./yr.)*

_____ _____

_____

Arm and Branch of Service:

_____

Highest Rank Achieved:

_____

Service Schools or Special Training:

_____

Languages or any other Special Skills:

_____

VII. References:
_____

Though the names of your references should NEVER be included in your résumé, it is a good idea to assemble all your data at the time you are preparing your résumé. Try to have a minimum of three people as references.

NOTE: Give complete address – street and number, city, state, and zip code. Give area code with telephone number.

Name of Reference: _____

Position: _____

Company Affiliation: _____

Company Address: _____

_____

Business Phone and Extension: _____

Name of Reference: _____

Position: _____

Company Affiliation: _____

Company Address: _____

_____

Business Phone and Extension: _____

Name of Reference: _____

Position: _____

Company Affiliation: _____

Company Address: _____

_____

Business Phone and Extension: _____

Name of Reference: _____

Position: _____

Company Affiliation: _____

Company Address: _____

_____

_____

Business Phone and Extension: _____

Name of Reference: _____

Position: _____

Company Affiliation: _____

Company Address: _____

_____

_____

Business Phone and Extension: _____

Name of Reference: _____

Position: _____

Company Affiliation: _____

Company Address: _____

_____

_____

Business Phone and Extension: _____

FOR EXPERIENCED WORKER WITH COLLEGE

I. Identifying Information:

Name: _____
If married woman, include married and maiden names.

Address: _____
Street and number, city, state, and zip code.

Home Phone: _____
Be sure to give area code.

Business Phone: _____
Be sure to give area code.

If business phone should be confidential, so state, i.e., Business phone: (212) 555-1280 (confidential).

II. Job Objective:

Remember – the job objective is OPTIONAL. If used, keep it brief. The only time it MUST be used is if you are trying to change careers.

_____

_____

_____

_____

III. Résumé Capsule:

The résumé capsule, like the job objective, is optional; however, one or the other must be used if you are trying to change careers.

_____

_____

_____

_____

_____

_____

IV. Employment History:

Your employment history should be listed in inverse chronological order.

Name of Company: _____

Address of Company: _____

_____

_____

Job Title: _____

Dates: Description of Responsibilities:

From   To
(mo./yr.)   (mo./yr.)

_____   _____

_____

_____

_____

_____

_____

_____

Name of Company: _____

Address of Company: _____

_____

_____

Job Title: _____

Dates: Description of Responsibilities:
From   *To*
(mo./yr.)   *(mo./yr.)*
_____   _____

                    _____

                    _____

                    _____

                    _____

                    _____

                    _____

Name of Company: _____

Address of Company: _____

                    _____

                    _____

Job Title: _____

Dates: Description of Responsibilities:
From   *To*
(mo./yr.)   *(mo./yr.)*
_____   _____

                    _____

                    _____

                    _____

                    _____

                    _____

                    _____

Name of Company: _____

Address of Company: _____

_____

_____

Job Title: _____

Dates: Description of Responsibilities:

From   *To*

(mo./yr.)   *(mo./yr.)*

_____   _____

_____

_____

_____

_____

V.   Educational History:

List your education as you did your employment history, IN INVERSE CHRONOLOGICAL ORDER. Your most advanced degree or your most recent education is first. Be sure to list all pertinent details – dates, degrees earned, educational institutions attended.

Advanced Degree:

Dates: Name of University:

From   *To*

(year)   *(year)*

_____   _____

Address of University:

_____

Degree Earned (or credits earned):

_____

Undergraduate Degree:

Dates:
From   To
(year)   (year)

_____

Name of College:

_____

Address of College:

_____

Degree Earned (or credits earned):

_____

Major: Minor:

_____   _____

VI. Personal Information:

Height: _____   Willing to Relocate: _____

Weight: _____   Willing to Travel: _____

Date of Birth: _____   Hobbies or Interests: _____

Marital Status: _____

Professional Memberships and Affiliations:

_____

_____

_____

_____

Publications and Major Achievements:

_____

_____

Military Service   (optional):

From   To
(mo./yr.)   (mo./yr.)

_____   _____

_____

Arm and Branch of Service:

_____

Highest Rank Achieved:

_____

'Service Schools or Special Training:

_____

Languages or any other Special Skills:

_____

VII.   References:

Though the names of your references should NEVER be included in your résumé, it is a good idea to assemble all your data at the time you are preparing your résumé. Try to have a minimum of three people as references.

NOTE: Give complete address – street and number, city, state, and zip code. Give area code with telephone number.

Name of Reference: _____

Position: _____

Company Affiliation: _____

Company Address: _____

_____

Business Phone and Extension: _____

Name of Reference: _____

Position: _____

Company Affiliation: _____

Company Address: _____

_____

Business Phone and Extension: _____

Name of Reference: _____

Position: _____

Company Affiliation: _____

Company Address: _____

_____

Business Phone and Extension: _____

Name of Reference: _____

Position: _____

Company Affiliation: _____

Company Address: _____

_____

Business Phone and Extension: _____

Name of Reference: _____

Position: _____

Company Affiliation: _____

Company Address: _____

_____

Business Phone and Extension: _____

Name of Reference: _____

Position: _____

Company Affiliation: _____

Company Address: _____

_____

Business Phone and Extension: _____

FOR ENTRY-LEVEL GRADUATE

I. Identifying Information:

Name: _____
If married woman, include married and maiden names.

Address: _____
Street and number, city, state, and zip code.

Home Phone: _____
Be sure to give area code.

Business Phone: _____
Be sure to give area code.

II. Job Objective:

Remember, the job objective is optional. If used, be brief and be sure that your stated objective does not limit your opportunities.

_____

_____

_____

_____

III. Educational Background:

Begin with your most advanced degree and, IN INVERSE CHRONOLOGICAL ORDER, list all degrees and certificates stopping with your bachelor's degree if you have attended college. In listing degrees and certificates give the name and address of the school along with the dates of attendence.

Dates: Name of School:
From   To
(year)   (year)
_____   _____

                           Address of School:

                           _____

                           Degree Earned (or credits earned):

                           _____

Major: Minor:

_____   _____

Dates:
(year to year)

Name of School:

_____

_____

Address of School:

_____

Degree Earned (or credits earned):

_____

Major: _____   Minor: _____

List all merit scholarships, awards, honors, including dates.

Scholarships:

_____

Awards:

_____

Honors:

_____

Class Standing or Grade Average (only list if noteworthy):

_____

List Extracurricular Activities, School Organizations, etc.:

_____

_____

_____

_____

_____

_____

IV. Employment History   (summer or part-time jobs)

Your employment history should be listed in inverse chronological order.

Name of Company: _____

Address of Company: _____

_____

_____

Job Title: _____

Dates: Description of Responsibilities:

From   *To*
(mo./yr.)   *(mo./yr.)*

_____   _____

_____

_____

_____

_____

_____

_____

_____

Name of Company: _____

Address of Company: _____

_____

_____

Job Title: _____

197

Dates:

From   *To*
(mo./yr.)   *(mo./yr.)*

Description of Responsibilities:

_____   _____

_____

_____

_____

_____

_____

Name of Company: _____

Address of Company: _____

_____

_____

Job Title: _____

Dates:

From   *To*
(mo./yr.)   *(mo./yr.)*

Description of Responsibilities:

_____   _____

_____

_____

_____

_____

_____

_____

Name of Company: _____

Address of Company: _____

_____

_____

Job Title: _____

Dates: Description of Responsibilities:
From   To
(mo./yr.)   (mo./yr.)

_____   _____

_____

_____

_____

_____

_____

_____

V. Other Skills and Abilities:

Languages (indicate degree of fluency — reading, speaking, writing):

_____

Typing (list speed in words per minute — w.p.m.):

_____

Steno (list speed in words per minute — w.p.m.):

_____

Bookkeeping (list familiarity with machines and calculators):

_____

Special Interests, Hobbies:

_____

_____

_____

_____

VI.   <u>Early Background:</u>

This is optional and should be used ONLY if there are factors in your background that are truly pertinent to your possible employment.

_____

_____

_____

_____

VII.   <u>References:</u>

Though the names of your references should NEVER be included in your résumé, it is a good idea to assemble all your data at the time you are preparing your résumé. Try to have a minimum of three people as references.

NOTE: Give complete address — street and number, city, state, and zip code. Give area code with telephone number.

Name of Reference: _____

Position: _____

Company Affiliation: _____

Company Address: _____

_____

Business Phone and Extension: _____

Name of Reference: _____

Position: _____

Company Affiliation: _____

Company Address: _____

_____

Business Phone and Extension: _____

Name of Reference: _____

Position: _____

Company Affiliation: _____

Company Address: _____

_____

Business Phone and Extension: _____

Name of Reference: _____

Position: _____

Company Affiliation: _____

Company Address: _____

_____

Business Phone and Extension: _____

Name of Reference: _____

Position: _____

Company Affiliation: _____

Company Address: _____

_____

Business Phone and Extension: _____

Name of Reference: _____

Position: _____

Company Affiliation: _____

Company Address: _____

_____

Business Phone and Extension: _____

VIII. Personal Information:

Height: _____   Marital Status: _____

Weight: _____   Willing to Relocate: _____

Date of Birth: _____   Willing to Travel: _____

Military Service (optional):

From   To
(mo./yr.)   (mo./yr.)

_____   _____

_____

Arm and Branch of Service: _

_____

Highest Rank Achieved:

_____

Service Schools or Special Training:

_____

Do's and Don'ts

On the preceding pages you've seen a great number of sample résumés. One of them may appeal to you as a good example to follow. Take your completed work sheets, along with the form of the résumé you've decided to use, and start writing. Don't be discouraged if the first few attempts are not completely satisfying. It may take several efforts before you complete the résumé that is right for you.

Possibly you have some original ideas of your own that you would like to work into your résumé. Go right ahead; but *please* be sure that you include all of the pertinent facts and adhere to the basic rules governing presentation and information. Below I have listed the do's and don'ts of résumé writing that are given to people who come to my agency.

- DO make it brief.

- DO include name and address in a conspicuous place.

- DO include all college degrees and dates received.

- DO list present work experience first, continuing in inverse chronological order.

- DO list all dates of employment with no unexplained gaps.

- DO give titles of jobs held and succinct accounts of duties.

- DO list major achievements such as publications and awards.

- DO list special skills and *fluent* foreign languages.

- DO NOT detail high school career (except special honors if you are a recent graduate).

- DO NOT give academic standing unless in upper 25 percentile, or grade average unless 3 points out of a possible 4.

- DO NOT list summer jobs unless you are a recent graduate or unless job is relevant to career choice.

- DO NOT include present salary or salary desired.

The balance of this chapter will be devoted to tips and suggestions. Usually the finishing touches of any work can make it or break it, and what we give here can help make your résumé.

- Use your typewriter to the fullest. Upper- and lower-case, underlining, tabulator keys for consistent indentation, asterisk key for separating sections, etc.

- Use at least half-inch margins on all four sides.

- Place dates so that they will stand out and can be compared easily.

- Skip a line or double space when changing to new subject in order to emphasize data.

- Check and double check your spelling; if in doubt about a word, refer to a dictionary.

- Avoid abbreviations except for degrees or titles.

- Use a new ribbon in your typewriter; it makes for easier reading and better reproduction.

- Clean typewriter keys.

- Use good bond or other quality paper.

- Use standard 8½″ × 11″ paper.

- Use a tinted paper, if you like, but stay with pale or pastel colors.

- Have copying done by a professional service and don't scrimp on cost.

On the following pages you will find sample layouts for your résumé. These are not meant to confine you to the models given, but rather to show the variation that is possible within the confines of the format for the chronological résumé, the style which I feel is the most effective. While the samples are all one page long, it should be pointed out that if you have to use two pages, it is preferable to have work history on one and educational background, personal data, hobbies, and such on the other. If you have to use two pages, they should be stapled together and on the bottom of the first page there should be a parenthetical indication that the résumé is continued on another page.

SAMPLE RÉSUMÉ — LAYOUT #1

Name
Street Address
City, State, Zip Code

Home Phone #
Business Phone #

Employment History

Job Title
From (date)   Name of Company
To present   Address of Company

Write out duties and responsibilities of job in question.

Job Title
From (date)   Name of Company
To (date)   Address of Company

Write out duties and responsibilities of job in question.

Job Title
From (date)   Name of Company
To (date)   Address of Company

Write out duties and responsibilities of job in question.

Educational History

From (date)   Name of College
To (date)   Address of College
                     Degree Earned

Personal Data   Hobbies

Height
Weight
Born (date)
Marital Status
Number of Children

References: On Request

Name   Height
Street Address   Weight
City, State, Zip Code   Date of Birth
Home Phone #   Marital Status
Business Phone #   Number of Children

Employment History

                              Job Title

From (date)   Name of Company
To present   Address of Company

                              Duties and responsibilities of job written out.

                              Job Title

From (date)   Name of Company
To (date)   Address of Company

                              Duties and responsibilities.

Educational History

From (date)   Name of College
To (date)   Address of College
                              Graduate Degree

From (date)   Name of College
To (date)   Address of College
                              Undergraduate Degree

References: Available on Request

Résumé of Qualifications

Name	Birth Date
Street Address	Height
City, State, Zip Code	Weight
Home Phone #	Marital Status
Business Phone #	Number of Children

Career Objective

To use the experience gained in . . .

Educational History

Name of College	From (date)
Address of College	To (date)
Advanced Degree	

Name of College	From (date)
Address of College	To (date)
Bachelor's Degree	

Employment History

Job Title

Name of Company	From (date)
Address of Company	To present

Description of duties and responsibilities in the above company.

Job Title

Name of Company	From (date)
Address of Company	To (date)

Description of duties and responsibilities in the company mentioned above.

Job Title

Name of Company	From (date)
Address of Company	To (date)

Description of duties and responsibilities.

References: Available on Request

SAMPLE RÉSUMÉ — LAYOUT #4

Resume of _____ *(name)* _____

Street Address   Date of Birth
City, State, Zip Code   Height
Home Phone #   Weight
Business Phone #   Marital Status

Employment History

Job Title
Name and Address of Company

Description of job, giving duties and responsibilities.

From (date) to present

Job Title
Name and Address of Company

Description of job.

From (date) to (date)

Educational History

Name and Address of College
Degree Received   From (date) to (date)

Hobbies

References:

Available on Request

SAMPLE RÉSUMÉ — LAYOUT #5

Resume of:

Name
_____

Street Address   Home Phone #
City, State, Zip Code   Business Phone #

Career Objective	To work as a ...
Employment History	
From (date) To present	Job Title — Name of Company Address of Company Description of duties and responsibilities in this job.
From (date) To (date)	Job Title — Name of Company Address of Company Description of responsibilities and duties in this position.
From (date) To (date)	Job Title — Name of Company Address of Company Description of nature of employment with duties and responsibilities.
Educational History	Degree — Name of College Address of College
Personal	Date of Birth; Height; Weight; Marital Status
References	Furnished on Request

Drafting Your Own Résumé

Note that these drafts are to be considered solely as models. You may wish to make deviations in your own résumé.

DRAFT WORKSHEETS FOR RECENT GRADUATES

Name _____

Street Address _____

City, State, Zip Code _____

Phone Number _____

Education

NOTE: *Education is listed in REVERSE chronological order (HIGHEST degree first). If you haven't attended and received a degree from a college, substitute high school.*

Date   Name of School _____

Degree Earned   Address of School _____

_____   Degree Earned _____

Date   Name of School _____

Degree Earned   Address of School _____

_____   Degree Earned _____

Dates _____   School Honors _____

Summer Experience

(Optional)   Job Objective _____

_____

Dates from
(mo./yr. — mo./yr.)

_____   Most recent employer _____

Address of employer _____

Job Title _____

Job Description _____

Dates from
(mo./yr. — mo./yr.)

_____   Next most recent employer _____

Address of employer _____

Job Title _____

Job Description _____

Personal

OPTIONAL

Hobby Information: _____

Personal History: _____

Information about Relocation: _____

Military Service: _____

Height: _____

Weight: _____

Birth Date: _____

Marital Status: _____

References upon request.

DRAFT WORKSHEETS FOR EXPERIENCED WORKERS

Name _____

Street Address _____

City, State, Zip Code _____

Home Phone: _____

Business Phone: _____

Experience

OPTIONAL

Job Objective _____

_____

Résumé Capsule _____

_____

Personal History _____

_____

NOTE: *Employers are listed in REVERSE chronological order.*

Dates:
From   To
(mo./yr.)   (mo./yr.)

_____   Most recent employer _____

Address of employer _____

Job Title _____

Job Description _____

Dates:
From   To
(mo./yr.)   (mo./yr.)

_____   Next most recent employer _____

Address of employer _____

Job Title _____

Job Description _____

Dates:
From   To
(mo./yr.) (mo./yr.)

_____   Next most recent employer _____

Address of employer _____

Job Title _____

Job Description _____

Dates:
From   To
(mo./yr.) (mo./yr.)

_____   Next most recent employer _____

Address of employer _____

Job Title _____

Job Description _____

Education
_____

*NOTE: Education is also listed in REVERSE chronological order (HIGHEST degree first).
If you haven't attended and received a degree from a college, substitute high school.*

Date   Name of School _____

Degree Earned   Address of School _____

_____   Degree Earned _____

Date   Name of School _____

Degree Earned   Address of School _____

_____   Degree Earned _____

Dates _____   School Honors _____

Personal

OPTIONAL

Hobby Information: _____

Personal History: _____

Publications: _____

Information about Relocation: _____

Military Service: _____

Height: _____

Weight: _____

Birth Date: _____

Marital Status: _____

References upon request.

Special Résumés

5

For Those Over Forty

If you are over forty, face it: there is no successful way of disguising the fact. Many "over-forties" think that if they omit *all* dates they can evade the issue of their age. Unfortunately, it doesn't work; the evasion merely emphasizes the fact that something is being hidden.

People in personnel, the résumé readers, tend to react adversely to résumés without dates, often to the extent of discarding them without giving them proper consideration. To be meaningful, a résumé must be factual. It must paint an accurate word picture of you. Résumés without dates simply are not informative, and as a result serve little useful purpose. They can even be counterproductive by creating the impression that you are much older than you really are, or by leading the reader to think that the lack of dates means that you are trying to hide a difficult-to-explain time gap in your history.

Some people advise that older people use a functional style résumé and omit all dates. But personnel people are not completely stupid. They are quick to recognize any résumé that tells only half a story, that looks as if it is being purposely evasive, and that is not completely straightforward. Usually such evasions only signal the very fact you are trying to hide. Such résumés waste both the reader's and the writer's time. Unless you are willing to be completely truthful in the presentation of your résumé, you may as well not bother to write it.

It really is a pity that so many mature people feel that their age is an insurmountable handicap. Whatever its drawbacks might be, it also has its advantages. Even if some employers are willing to spend time and effort in training an inexperienced young person, others vastly prefer to hire the almost instant productivity that an experienced, mature person can offer.

Our advice to the "over forty" is simple: in preparing your résumé, follow your chosen format and put in all the appropriate dates. Be proud of your age and experience. State the facts truthfully and with dignity. Preparing your résumé may take a little longer than it would a younger person, but you will ultimately find a completely satisfying job.

John Spring
26 Waverly Place
Hastings, New York 13076
Phone: 914-261-1234

Career Objective: To secure either a part- or full-time
                    position to augment my retirement
                    pension.

Experience

1950-1978   U.S. Post Office
            White Plains, New York
            Postmaster

Education

1944-1949   Commercial High School
            White Plains, New York
            Commercial diploma

Personal

Born: August 2, 1923
Height: 5'8"
Weight: 190 lbs.
Marital Status: Widower

References on request.

For Minorities

At this time, most employers, being very conscious of the image they present to the public (and of the anti-discrimination laws), are doing their utmost to avoid any hiring practice that could be interpreted as discriminatory against minorities. Often, as a result of this, previous employment practices are being reversed. Today, a member of a minority who has a good educational background and/or work history is likely to be given preference in being hired.

Nonetheless, I suggest that you try neither to emphasize nor conceal your minority background. Listing it as an item under personal data could work to your disadvantage, as it might appear as defiance. Best would be to treat it as a matter of course. If you belong to any organizations or professional societies that would indicate your belonging to a minority, you could list them under the appropriate heading.

For the Returning Housewife

To be fully prepared, the returning housewife, like all other job seekers, must have a résumé. Its general format would be the same as any other résumé. Like any other résumé, it must account for all time, even though ten or fifteen years were spent pursuing the functions and responsibilities of a wife and/or mother.

After the introductory identifying information, the job objective or career goal, if it is used, would be stated. This would be followed by the dates that were spent at home. The "employment history" for that period can mention, as simply as possible, the functions of keeping house and raising children. This would be glossed over briefly, but *it is of extreme importance* to include any volunteer work such as PTA or fund-raising in which you were involved.

Never underestimate the value of your volunteer work. Not only has it helped an important cause, but properly described, it will be a very valuable asset to your marketability. The very fact that you have done volunteer work can tell a prospective employer much about your abilities and interests.

If you have been an administrator for any non-profit organization, it will be assumed immediately that you can offer the same talents to any employer searching for someone to accept managerial responsibilities. Only a short time ago, one of my agency's clients asked us to recruit a mature person with managerial potential to take on the supervision of a market research group. The person hired would have to direct a staff of interviewers, interview and hire new employees for this market research function, and coordinate all of their interviews. The person would have to be well-organized and have a background that manifests managerial abilities.

Several of my placement counselors were busy reading résumés to find such a person. Ideally we were looking for a returnee whose résumé showed extensive volunteer administrative experience. We were aware, of course, that many of the people whose résumés we had rejected might have had such experience, but since the information wasn't included in the résumé, we could not, in good conscience, ask our client to give them consideration.

Many of our returnees' résumés point out interesting and salable talents acquired in voluntary work. Such skills as writing a non-profit organization's newsletter, organizing fund-raising events, working with the handicapped, door-to-door soliciting of contributions, and other similar volunteer activities show abilities and talents that are very valuable on the job market.

In listing your volunteer experience, as in your employment history, list all activities with dates. If you were responsible for any special projects, be sure to describe them with the importance they deserve.

Your past employment history, even though fifteen years may have elapsed, should be noted. Give dates, job titles, and responsibilities. Be sure to list any skills such as stenography, typing, bookkeeping, etc. Even if they are a bit rusty, such skills are very useful to prospective employers.

Your educational history should be included in the same manner as it is with any other job applicant. You must realize that even people who have been working consistently for the past fifteen years continue to list their college degrees. If you have received a graduate degree and kept up, through journals or books, with the material in your field, this should be mentioned.

Do not be disheartened. I would never claim that a returnee would find work without encountering any difficulty whatsoever. But work *is* available and there are many employers who appreciate the qualities — stability, respect for the work ethic, willingness to accept responsibility — that a returnee obviously can offer.

A returnee's résumé, like any other, should not be sent out without a covering letter. The covering letter should clearly and unequivocally state that provisions for taking care of the home and of any young children have been made. There is no need to go into any detail concerning the nature of those provisions. (See the sample on page 243.)

It is understandable that an employer would have some concern about the seriousness of a returnee's intentions of remaining at work, but these doubts are not going to be dispelled by a detailed explanation of plans that have been made for care of young children. In addition, you must recognize that employers often look for what they consider to be the most gentle way of refusing to hire someone. They are liable to think it is more brutal to say, "I'm sorry, but you don't have what we're looking for," than to tell you, "We'd like to hire you, but we're afraid you'll be concentrating on your home rather than the job."

Furthermore, you are entitled to some degree of privacy. A married man with three children is not questioned about the care of the children. Nor is he asked whether he would be able to continue working if something should happen (or has happened) to his wife.

Habits die hard, unfortunately, and some employers still cling to the belief that a mother with dependent children is an employment risk. Your protestations to the contrary will be useless with such people. There is a way, however, of demonstrating that you are not a risk. That is by taking temporary employment before looking for a permanent job.

Working as a "temp" for a month or two is an excellent idea for a returnee. It serves a threefold purpose: it gives you time to iron out home problems; it gives you a chance to polish up rusty skills; and it gives you a recent reference proving that your home doesn't interfere with your job. Not only would you want to be able to put those two or three months of temporary work into your résumé, but you would also want to mention them in your covering letter — they could be the factor that would tip the scales in your favor.

MODEL RÉSUMÉ FOR THE RETURNING HOUSEWIFE

Martha Smith Harley
35 Ridge Street
Scarsdale, New York 10583

Home Phone: 914–SC3–0012
Marital Status: Married
Date of Birth: May 2, 1930
Height: 5'5"
Weight: 130 lbs.

1960 — Present	Housewife and Mother

Volunteer Work

Nurse's Aide
St. John's Hospital
Yonkers, New York

Fund-Raising Volunteer
Easter Seals Campaign

President
P. T. A.

1954 — 1960   **Executive Secretary**

John T. Peters
Public Relations Consultant
286 Lexington Avenue
New York, New York 10016

Secretarial duties included client contact,
setting up meetings, travel arrangements, full
use of steno and typing, and editing press
releases. Also handled routine correspondence,
light bookkeeping and switchboard relief.

1948 — 1954   **Stenographer**

United City Bank
320 West 36th Street
New York, New York 10036

Member of stenographic pool. Took dictation
and transcribed it. Worked for ten executives.

1944 — 1948   Yonkers Commercial High School
Yonkers, New York

Received diploma in commercial studies.

For the Handicapped

A very effective and convincing publicity campaign, consisting not only of paid advertisements, but of news stories as well, has done much to alleviate the problems the handicapped have previously had in finding employment. Employers are coming to recognize that many of the fears they had about employing handicapped people are not only unjustified, but are demonstrably false. Studies conducted over recent years have shown that, as a group, handicapped people suffer less from absenteeism, are involved in fewer work-related accidents, and are more productive than the average worker without a handicap. Some companies, recognizing the benefits accruing from hiring the handicapped, are even modifying offices and plants in order to remove physical obstacles to employment of the handicapped.

A handicapped person's résumé would not differ in any respect from any other person's résumé. It serves the same function: it is a summary of the educational background and work history of an applicant, listing his or her qualifications and assets. As such, it is not the place to discuss a handicap as a problem or as an impediment to employment.

While we do not feel that a handicap should be mentioned in a résumé, we do feel that it should be briefly discussed in a covering letter. This is consistent with our belief that being straightforward and completely honest is always the best approach to employment "problems." The personnel director of a large advertising agency, in answer to my agency's queries concerning the matter of *not* mentioning a handicap prior to the interview, said, "The fewer surprises in an interview, the better." In reply to the same question, another personnel director told us, "It's like meeting someone whose résumé fits a job's specification perfectly, and then learning he speaks only Chinese."

The reality is that certain jobs are obviously closed to people suffering from specific handicaps, but there are many jobs that any handicapped person *can* fill. A few years ago, my agency received a résumé from a woman who was recently graduated from Cornell University. Her résumé indicated that she had majored in history and minored in English, achieving a 3.24 grade-point average over four years. Her covering letter indicated that she was deaf, but that she hoped that this would not prove to be too great a liability.

As we were impressed by her résumé, we replied and suggested she come to us for a screening interview. When she arrived at our offices, it was obvious that she was not only intelligent, but that she had a very realistic attitude toward her disability. We encountered no difficulty in placing her with a large textbook publisher as a copyeditor trainee. The last news we have had from her was that she was assistant editor of the firm's American history division.

Although her deafness would have disqualified her for any position requiring phone work, it was not a liability for a position requiring proofreading, research, and editing. This should be borne in mind when you are writing your covering letter. It should be similar to any other covering letter in stating your reasons for applying to that particular company and in indicating those points in your résumé that would be of special interest to that company. Only at the very end would you describe briefly your physical handicap. (See the sample on page 244.)

Remember: In your covering letter your lead should be your assets – not your disability.

MODEL RÉSUMÉ FOR THE HANDICAPPED

NOTE: *Nothing should appear on the résumé about the handicap, but it should be mentioned in the covering letter.*

Dorothy Rogers
36 Washington Place
Augusta, Maine 09876
Home phone: (207) 456-1324

Personal Information:	Born: **7-2-49**　Height: **5'5"**　Weight: **115**　Status: **Single**
Career Objective:	Entry-level position in communications industry
Education:	Received B.A., June, 1969 Cornell University Ithaca, New York *Major:*　History *Minor:*　English Graduated with honors.　Average 3.4
Extracurricular Activities:	Editor of college literary magazine 1967–1969
Employment History:	**Typist —** Glacy, Inc., Ithaca, New York — Summer, 1968 **Typist —** Marci, Inc., Ithaca, New York — Summer, 1967 **File Clerk —** A. Flor & Co., Ithaca, New York — Summer, 1966
Skills:	Type at a speed of 65 words per minute
Interests:	Reading, cooking and skiing
References:	References will be provided on request

Changing for the Better

In every moment of every day, someone, somewhere, feeling as if he or she is on a treadmill going nowhere, is pondering a complete and radical change of career. Someone else, either laid-off or phased-out, feels that the answer to his or her employment problems is in a field different from the previous one. Whatever the reason, be it choice or necessity, the techniques of a career change are much the same.

The decision should not be capricious. You have to give serious consideration to your prospects, and make an honest evaluation of your abilities and talents before you can even attempt to change your career. You will have to read your résumé carefully and note which of your skills, interests, and previous responsibilities are appropriate to other fields. You are planning to exchange the commitment and expertise you have acquired in one area for the opportunity to prove your abilities in a new field.

I have often seen an attorney become an editor, an engineer become a sales manager, and an executive secretary become an administrator. Teachers usually have a talent for personnel counseling; journalists have much to offer a corporate public relations department; and architects can become superlative display designers. My agency has placed ex-pilots in sales programs, and once placed a nun who had left the convent—we found her a job counseling students in an international student exchange program.

Once you have decided to change fields and have picked an area that will find your qualifications attractive, you are ready to write your new résumé. While basically the same as the one you used for your original field, it has one important difference. The job objective or career goal is *not* optional and you must include it as well as a capsule résumé. In this manner you explain what sort of work you are seeking as well as how your past experience qualifies you for it.

For instance, if your background is in engineering and you want to change to a career in technical writing, you simply state your goal in your job objective, i.e.,

> *Job Objective:* An opportunity as a technical writer that would use the expertise acquired in ten years as a professional engineer.

The career goal is followed by the same information you would have included in a résumé written for your original field. It is important to remember that your new résumé must be truthful as well as logical. Once again—never put anything in your résumé that is not completely honest. Stay with the truth even if you feel that a small exaggeration or distortion might make you more marketable. Any information that is not true can become an irremediable liability. Employers are willing to train you in areas where you are weak, but not if you had claimed strength in that area. The latter is more likely to result in your loss of the job.

A teacher wishing to start a new career in counseling or personnel should write a complete résumé giving the teaching background, but before the work history, a *combined* job objective and capsule résumé should be inserted:

> *Job Objective:* A career in personnel or counseling which would utilize ten years of dealing with students and parents while a teacher.

A newspaper writer looking for a career in public relations uses the same format. The *combined* résumé capsule/job objective might read like this:

> *Job Objective:* A position in public relations which can utilize the facility in writing and the sense of newsworthiness that has come from 12 years of newspaper work.

We recently interviewed a research biologist who wanted to change his field to public opinion research. He enjoyed research, but felt that his present work was too restricted and wanted to be more involved with work directly affecting human behavior. We discussed his résumé and decided that merely by rewriting his job objective, the résumé he already had prepared would serve his purpose excellently:

> *Job Objective:* To employ in the field of public opinion research the broad knowledge of statistical techniques gained in six years' work in biological research.

Or an editor wanting to leave the publishing field:

> *Job Objective:* A position where my background as an editor of elementary and high school texts can be used in the areas of sales or marketing.

For the Foreign-Born

The question of whether to include in your résumé the fact that you are foreign born and a U.S. citizen is best answered by analyzing whether such information will add to your marketability. If so, you should include it; if not, there's no point in mentioning it.

If you were born in another country and, therefore, are completely fluent in a foreign language, by all means mention it. Your language ability will often be of interest to an employer. Knowledge of foreign languages is especially useful to many companies, since so much business has become international; fluency in a second language is an asset, and should always be included in your résumé.

A short while ago, a major law firm was recruiting recent college graduates for training positions as paralegals. Though they had not expressed a need for competence in French, they were very impressed with one résumé that mentioned that this candidate was born and raised in France, and was completely fluent in French. The law firm was interested in this candidate because they had offices in Paris, and would benefit by an employee who could not only be trained as a legal assistant, but could also become involved with their foreign branches.

On the other hand, if you were born abroad and didn't acquire any additional skills as a result, there's no need in mentioning your birth place in your résumé. Résumé readers are interested only in what you can offer them in terms of experience and abilities — not in personal background information about you.

If you have immigrated to the U.S. as a mature individual, already having had education and employment in your native land, list that information in the same manner as you would any other.

If you had difficulty in your native country because of political reasons, and did not work because of this for any period of time, state that fact as an explanation for what would otherwise be an unaccountable lapse of time in your employment history.

MODEL RÉSUMÉ FOR THE FOREIGN-BORN PERSON WITH LANGUAGE SKILLS

Lee D. Sofson
53 Fern Avenue
Greensboro, N. C. 28615

(714) 287–4908

CAREER OBJECTIVE

To manage a large-volume general bookstore, and/or act in a major buying capacity. Willing to relocate; prefer Northeast, Northwest, or West Coast.

EXPERIENCE

June 1973 to present	**Store Manager** – B. Beeton Bookseller, Asheville, North Carolina. Present sales volume $432,000+ (21% above goal); selling cost less than 2% of budgeted payroll; inventory shortage less than 2% for year. Sales increased during past year 25%.
February, 1973 to June, 1973	**Manager Trainee** – B. Beeton Bookseller, Atlanta, Georgia. At time of training, this store was the largest volume store in the chain (sales per-square-foot).
February, 1972 to present	**Free-Lance Writer** – *Soul & Jazz, down beat, Changes* – Interest in contemporary jazz has led to record reviews, interviews, and articles for these and other magazines. Am a staff writer for *Soul & Jazz,* 6922 Hollywood Boulevard, Los Angeles, California. Bill Chappell/Associate Publisher.
May, 1971 to February, 1972	**Sales Clerk** – Record Bar, Inc., Athens, Georgia, and Music Grotto, Athens, Georgia. Was a sales clerk for both these nationwide retail music stores.

EDUCATION	University of Georgia. Graduated in 1971.
SPECIAL SKILLS	**Tri-lingual:** English – German – French Born and lived in Switzerland until 1967.
PROFESSIONAL AFFILIATIONS	Member of ABA. Certified completion of ABA/NACS Booksellers School, 1974.
REFERENCES	Complete references will be furnished on request.

MODEL RÉSUMÉ FOR THE FOREIGN-BORN PERSON WITHOUT LANGUAGE SKILLS

Roy Allen Samco   Home Phone: (201) 276-6314
43 Pinewood Crescent
Englewood, New Jersey 07614

Employment

May 1973 to present   Prentice-Hall, Inc.
                                 Englewood Cliffs, New Jersey 07632

Currently Special Projects Copywriter in the College Advertising Department. Duties: Write and edit copy, design layouts for priority and high-budget brochures, catalogs, and journal advertisements.

Promoted to present position from the Journal Advertising Department, where duties involved writing copy, designing layouts, and producing journal ads for various journals. In addition, assigned, edited, and coordinated all journal ads in the College Advertising Department.

Original position in the company was as a copywriter/designer, also in the College Advertising Department. Functions involved writing copy, designing layouts, and producing direct mail brochures, journal ads, letters, and posters.

Possess extensive knowledge of production, type, and layout. Work closely with artists, photographers, printers, marketing managers, editors, and authors. Have trained new copywriters, giving them concepts of writing and the mechanics needed to produce various ads and/or brochures.

In addition, have performed freelance work (copy and layout) for our Educational Book Division, and for a small, independent publisher.

Education

1971 – 1974   Graduate courses in English at the University of Scranton and at
                                 Seton Hall University in South Orange, New Jersey. M.A.,
                                 December 1974.

1967 – 1971   University of Scranton, Scranton, Pennsylvania.
                                 Major: English with a Minor in Philosophy. Received B.A. in English
                                 May 1971.

1963 – 1967   Saint Benedict's Preparatory School, Newark, New Jersey.
                                 College Preparatory Program.

Awards and Honors

1970 – 1971   Dean's Honor List at the University of Scranton.

Personal Data   Date of Birth: May 11, 1949.

References   Will be furnished upon request.

MODEL RÉSUMÉ FOR THE FOREIGN-BORN PERSON — POLITICAL REFUGEE

Milton Cinajbah
231 East 87th Street
New York, New York 10023
Home phone: (212) 862-8064

Editorial Experience

1972 — 1973	Yugoslav News Agency "Tanjug" correspondent from Latin America. Based in Rio de Janeiro. Coverage of Brazil, Argentina, Uruguay, Paraguay, Guyana and Surinam.
1969 — 1972	Yugoslav News Agency "Tanjug" Chief Editor of Slovene Bureau, with coverage of neighboring European countries Austria, Hungary, Italy and assignments in other Western European countries.
1964 — 1969	Chief Editor of Belgrade Bureau of the *Vjesnik u Srijedu* news magazine (leading Yugoslav magazine published in Zagreb, with circulation of over 500 thousand) with longer assignments in Italy, Holland, Germany, etc.
1959 — 1964	Correspondent of Zagreb-based weekly newsmagazine *Globus* in Belgrade. Promoted to chief of Bureau in 1961.

Education

From third grade of elementary school on, attended English language schools in the U.S. and Rome, Italy. Graduated from the Anglo-American "Overseas School of Rome" in 1954.

Degree in Comparative World Literature and English from Belgrade University in 1961.

Languages

Full knowledge of Slovene, English, Italian, Serbo-Croatian. Fluent in Portuguese and to a lesser extent in Spanish. Working knowledge (translation) of French.

Related Experience

For ten years wrote regularly the most widely read food column in Yugoslavia, in the *Vjesnik u Srijedu* and *Weekend* magazines, both with sales of over half a million.

Two years' experience as scenarist and assistant director in documentary films from 1958 to 1960.

Personal

Age 45. Married. In the United States as a political refugee.

References Upon Request

For the Returning Service Person

If you are returning from military service, you will, like everyone else, need an up-to-date résumé in order to land a good job.

Your military service should be treated as a period of employment and should occupy the most prominent position on your résumé. If you decide to use a career or job objective (remember, its use is optional), it should be followed *immediately* by a concise description of your military career. If you do not use a job objective, the description of your military service must contain the following information:

1. Date (year and month) you became associated with the military,
2. Date (year and month) you left the military,
3. Arm and branch of service,
4. The highest rank received and military occupational specialty,
5. Any service schools attended,
6. Special training,
7. Places you were stationed.

It's a good idea to use the work sheets provided on pages 180 to 202 and be sure you have all your facts absolutely correct before you start writing your résumé.

After the summary of your military career, you should follow one of the general résumé formats on pages 205 to 209 listing, in reverse chronological order, your education and work history. For example, if you joined the military service right after you graduated from college, you should place your educational summary immediately after the description of your service history. If, however, you were employed right before you joined the military service, the description of your work history (in reverse chronological order) should follow the data about your military association.

Bear in mind that the duties involved in any given military occupational specialty might not be known to a civilian. For instance, many civilians may not be aware that a Company Master Sergeant is primarily a managerial office worker whose major concerns are assignments of duties, maintenance of schedules, and supervision of other office workers such as company clerks, supply sergeants, and supply clerks.

Such experience in the military can easily be translated to any administrative or supervisory job opportunity.

EUGENE RAFFERTY
300 North Riverside Drive
Nashville, Tennessee 23456
(615) 753-1234

JOB OBJECTIVE

To secure a management trainee position with a large company.

MILITARY SERVICE

June, 1973 to June, 1978

U. S. Navy

Apprentice Seaman
promoted to
Seaman 1st Class
Stationed in Alaska
Honorably discharged

EXPERIENCE

August, 1971 to May, 1973

Management Trainee — W.T. Grant, Nashville, Tennessee
Duties included waiting on customers in every department of the store,
operating the cash registers, assisting in the stock room and keeping track
of merchandise in stock.

EDUCATION

1967 — 1971
Nashville Commercial High School
Nashville, Tennessee

PERSONAL

Born 2/2/53   6'2"   190 pounds   Single

HOBBIES

Bowling, Swimming, Camping

REFERENCES

References on request

Since neither past salaries nor new minimum salaries should ever be discussed in your résumé, the desire for a jump in salary must be implied rather than stated. Remember, the purpose of the résumé is to elicit enough interest in you to get an interview, and it's only at that interview that your salary requirements should be discussed.

HOW SHALL I IMPLY I WANT MORE MONEY?

If your résumé shows that you are presently employed, the reader will infer that you are probably interested in a new job because you are looking for an opportunity that will offer a higher salary. In other words, it will be written as any other résumé where the writer is currently employed.

If, however, you are looking for an increase in responsibility as well as in salary, that fact can be easily stated in your job application.

For example, if you are an Assistant Publicity Director and are seeking a new position as Publicity Director, both facts should appear in your résumé.

Your new goal should appear in the Job or Career Objective and your present (or past) job title should be included in your employment history. For example:

Job Objective: Publicity Director
(Present or last employment): Assistant Publicity Director

When looking for a higher (or different) level job than you've held before, you *must* use a Job Objective. The Job Objective here is *not* optional; it must be used because it is the only way to explain what you are looking for and why it is logical that you are qualified for such a position.

Thomas Josephs
435 Drew Street
Cleveland, Ohio 44135
Home Phone: (216) 349-4561

Career Objective: Production Supervisor in field of Metallurgy

June 1972 to   **Assistant Production Supervisor**
February 1979   Crane Metal, Inc.
                      Cleveland, Ohio

Assisted in the supervision of six engineers, three lot technicians and four production workers. Was involved with metallurgical aspects of high speed tool steels emphasizing salt bath and atmosphere control heat treating, nitriding, and tempering; incoming steel quality control checks including Chemical, Metallography, and Physical Metallurgy; quality control experience involving statistics and future production requirements, troubleshooting customer complaints with respect to both metallurgical and non-metallurgical process deviations; ordering all necessary supplies vital to heat treating; R and D for implementation of processes involving cost reduction.

August 1967   **Metallurgic Engineer**
to May 1972   Windsor Steel Company
                      Pittsburgh, Pennsylvania

Involved with metallurgical aspects of cold extrusion including metal defect reduction, non-destructive testing, chemical analysis, development and/or modification and implementation of processes involving statistics, control charts, and capabilities with respect to both metallurgical and non-metallurgical process deviations.

EDUCATION

1963 to 1967   B. S. Metallurgical Engineering
                      University of Pittsburgh
                      Pittsburgh, Pennsylvania

PERSONAL

Date of birth: 1-6-45   *Height:* 6' 2"
Weight: 160 lbs.   *Marital Status:* Married

"Promotion" Résumés

How to write your résumé to show you've been continually promoted:

A résumé depicting your job career in any company can be very effective if done correctly. Suppose you've been employed for ten years with the X Company. You started in 1966 as an Accounts Payable Clerk; two years later (1968), you were promoted to Assistant Bookkeeper; then, in 1974, you again received a promotion, this time to your present job as Full-Charge Bookkeeper/Office Manager.

A very interesting résumé can be written if you examine each job category individually, detailing it with dates, job titles, and descriptions. Your present or last job title is listed first and, in reverse chronological order, each descending position.

Several examples are given on the following pages.

MODEL "PROMOTION" RÉSUMÉ #1

Rosemary Hutt
62 Marsh Street
Chicago, Illinois 60602

Home Phone: (312) 324-6509
Business Phone: (312) 543-2367
Birth Date: March 7, 1942
Marital Status: Single
Height: 5'7"
Weight: 118 lbs.

Job Objective: To continue a career as acquisitions editor in educational publishing.

1964 — present   **CHARNEY PUBLISHING, INC.**
400 Landen Street
Chicago, Illinois 60634

1970 — present   **Acquisitions Editor**
College Division of
Charney Publishing, Inc.

As acquisitions editor, assigned and developed over 150 new books while
managing a list of 500 titles which grossed about five million dollars annually.
Disciplines of Mathematics, Engineering, Physics, and Chemistry.

1966 — 1970   **District Sales Manager**
Charney Publishing, Inc.

Territory: Arizona, Utah, and Nevada.
Responsibilities included management of six sales representatives. Was responsible
for 3.6 million dollar annual revenue. In this four-year period, revenues increased
by twenty percent.

1964 — 1966   **Field Sales Representative**
Charney Publishing, Inc.

Territory: Arizona, Utah, and Nevada
Functioned as Math, Chemistry, and Physics Specialist, calling on colleges,
universities, and junior colleges. Was responsible for 3/4-million dollars revenue.
In this two-year period, sales increased by 22%.

1960 — 1964   University of New Hampshire
Durham, New Hampshire

B. A. Degree

References furnished on request.

June Tracey
65 West Main Street
Geneva, New York 20318
315 — 625-5674

Date of Birth: May 5, 1950
Height: 5'9"
Weight: 142 lbs.
Marital Status: Married
No children

Career Objective: Responsible position as an Administrative Assistant.

EXPERIENCE

February 1974
to present

Secretary to Advertising Manager — Universal Enterprises, Geneva, New York. Serve as personal and confidential secretary, handling all correspondence — both personal and business, filing, telephone contacts, appointments, etc.; detailed follow-up on work in progress, supervise department staff; handle all public relations and advertising, including writing and placing of ads in newspapers and trade magazines.

July 1971 to
December 1973

Secretary — PDA Films, Geneva, New York. As a secretary to the producer, was responsible for typing scripts, taking notes at writers' meetings as well as the usual Gal Friday responsibilities. Scheduled rehearsal meetings, liaison with client and advertising agencies.

EDUCATION   Marymount College, New York.
Major: English.   Minors: History and Political Science.
B.A., June 1971.

SKILLS   Shorthand — 90 w.p.m.   Typing — 70 w.p.m.
Knowledge of adding machines, calculators, various duplicating machines (Xerox, IBM, etc.), addressograph, and telex.

REFERENCES   Provided on request.

The Covering Letter

6

A covering letter should be enclosed whenever you send your résumé to a prospective employer. While it rarely gives any information that is not included in your résumé, its enclosure is an act of courtesy and a sign of a serious and professional approach to job hunting. It gives each employer you approach an indication of personal attention that would not be shown by the arrival of an unaccompanied résumé.

It makes no difference whether you are sending the résumé in answer to an ad or as part of your personal mailing campaign; the covering letter will always follow the same simple rules. It should be brief, limited to one page, and of no more than four paragraphs. Unlike the résumé, it should never be reproduced, but always individually typed. Needless to say, it should be neatly typed and conform to the standards of business correspondence.

Whenever possible, the letter should be addressed to a particular individual in the company, preferably by name. If you cannot ascertain the name, address the letter to the personnel director, or, by title, to the head of the department that you are hoping to work in. In answering an ad, however, address your letter as the ad indicates. If this is nothing more than a box number, don't try to guess the title of the person who will be first to see your résumé.

Your first paragraph of the covering letter should tell why you are writing to that particular company. If it is in answer to an ad, you so state, and give the name and date of the publication where the ad appeared. If a friend who is an employee of the company has suggested you apply, you should give the name, title or job category, and department where employed. If writing as part of your own mail campaign, you should explain in two or three lines why work with that particular company interests you.

The following one or two paragraphs should point out the salient features of your résumé that could be of interest to your correspondent. These could be features in either your educational background or your work history. In certain circumstances, you could elaborate slightly on one or two details of your résumé. For example, if your résumé simply states that you worked as circulation manager of a newspaper, your letter could add the information that circulation increased by 43 percent in the six years you worked there as a direct result of a program that you developed. But again, whatever is said should be said briefly.

The last paragraph should be a closing, indicating your hope that you have created interest in yourself and suggesting further communication to arrange an interview.

As your covering letter is used to highlight certain aspects of your résumé, the same résumé can be used to pursue different job opportunities. The covering letter, stressing your most appropriate skills and talents, can be geared to each particular company that will be the recipient of your résumé. Not only does this immediately call attention to your possible value to that company, but it *personalizes* the letter and makes it clear that it is not a simple form letter sent out with each copy of your résumé.

From our observations, we have come to believe that a covering letter accompanying a résumé does get more attention from recruiters and personnel people than does an unaccompanied résumé.

MODEL COVERING LETTER NO. 1 — REPLY TO ADVERTISEMENT

29 Ridge Road
Elmira, New York 10623
April 14, 1978

Box X3349
New York Guardian
749 East 56th Street
New York, New York 10022

Dear Sir:

I am replying to your advertisement of this date offering a position as copy editor on a sports car publication.

As my resume demonstrates, I have my B.S. in journalism and have been working as copy writer and assistant copy editor on magazines for the past six years.

Your ad specified an interest in and knowledge of sports cars. I did not feel it appropriate to mention it in my resume, but I am the owner of one of the few surviving Type 57 Bugattis in this country, and have rebuilt and maintain the car myself. The car is registered with the Bugatti Club of America to which I also belong. I hope this establishes my credentials as a sports car enthusiast.

If my background is of use to you, please contact me at your convenience.

I appreciate your consideration.

Yours truly,

Anthony Lo Bello

Encl.

16 Chilton Street
Cleveland, Ohio 40612
April 9, 1978

Mr. George Teasdale
Personnel Manager
United Chemical Corporation
452 Sorrent Drive
Teeterboro, New Jersey 11402

Dear Mr. Teasdale:

I am replying to your advertisement in the April issue of
Cosmetic Chemistry.

While having no specific background in cosmetic chemistry,
I would like to point out that my work with Basic Pharmaceutical's Anesthetic and Analgesic division consisted primarily of
developing and testing non-oleaginous bases for topical anes-
thetics. The basis, of course, had to be broadly anti-allergic
if they were to be of commercial value and were tested for same.
Our procedures, in both development and testing, were similar
to those used in the cosmetic industry, and our tests were at
least as rigorous.

My résumé also shows, as your ad requested, heavy Quantita-
tive Analysis and Quality Control experience.

I would like to speak with you further. I will be in New
York for the Pharmaceutical Chemists' Society meeting next
month. Could we arrange an interview for that time?

Thank you for your consideration.

Yours truly,

John Villiers

Enclosure

320 Garrity Drive
Chicago, Illinois   11625
May 24, 1978

Mr. Henry Wilford
President
Seafarer's Museum
Xenobia, Maine   10874

Dear Mr. Wilford:

I am applying for a position with your Museum as I feel my experience
in developing a Museum Sales Department will be of interest to you.

As my résumé indicates, I held the position as Sales Manager of Wood-
bury Reconstruction Company for six years. In this capacity, I
developed a mail order sales department and created a successful book-
shop specializing in native crafts.

I expect to be in the vicinity of Xenobia in the first week of July.
Could we arrange for an interview at that time? As I am currently
employed, I would appreciate this be kept in confidence.

Your consideration is greatly appreciated.

Sincerely yours,

Richard Shelton

Enclosure

474 Hardscrabble Road
Millville, New York 10901
April 4, 1978

Ms. Bernice Luddington
Art Director
Abington's Department Store
1502 Mamaroneck Avenue
White Plains, New York 10603

Dear Ms. Luddington:

The controller of your Paramus branch, William Scott, who is a neighbor of mine, has told me that you have an opening for a display designer in your White Plains Store.

As you can see from my résumé, I had extensive experience in the field prior to the birth of my first child. While I have been unable to seek employment in the field for several years, I have kept my hand in, as it were, by designing displays of art and handicrafts as a volunteer at our local library.

My youngest child is now in high school and able to take care of himself. In addition, my sister lives nearby and has agreed to take care of any emergency that might arise; so, I will be able to devote myself whole-heartedly to my job.

I would welcome an opportunity to speak with you. Could I call your secretary for an appointment?

Thank you for your consideration.

Yours sincerely,

Helen Fries

Enclosure

19 Wingate Road
Cleveland, Ohio 12345
November 6, 1978

Miss Irene Gaines
Personnel Manager
Morgan and Stern
425 Sunsent Drive
Cleveland, Ohio 12346

Dear Miss Gaines:

I am replying to your advertisement for a legal secretary which appeared in the November 3 issue of *The Cleveland Star*.

As my résumé shows, I had six years of consistent secretarial experience from 1966-1972 and have always had an interest in being employed by a law firm.

I have been home for the past four years with my two young children but feel I am ready to return to the business world.

I have recently employed a "live-in" college student and am convinced my children and home responsibilities are properly taken care of.

I would like very much to meet you and am available at any time convenient to you.

Sincerely yours,

Mary Lienda

Enclosure

14 Riverview Drive
Syracuse, New York   12343
March 25, 1979

Mr. William Jacobson
Hall and Hall, Inc.
964 West 44 Street
New York, New York   10032

Dear Mr. Jacobson:

As you can see by the enclosed résumé, I will be graduating
this May from Cornell University and am interested in finding an
entry level position in either book or magazine publishing.

Though my long range goals are in the area of copyediting and
proofreading, I am completely realistic about the nature of entry
level positions. I type 70 wpm and would be quite ready to start
as a secretary or Guy Friday.

I wish to be frank and mention that I have been deaf since
birth though I am adept at both lip reading and sign language.

I expect to be in New York City during Easter vacation, April
18 to 25. I will get in touch with you before Easter in hope of
scheduling an interview.

Looking forward to meeting you.

Cordially,

Martin Thomas

Enclosure

Getting to Know Yourself

In order to be successful in your job search, it is imperative that you really know what you are looking for. Knowledge of the job market, an effective résumé, introduction to a superior list of employers — all great assets in any job campaign — will not help you if you are basically unaware of your real interests and motivations.

It is well worth the time and effort to spend a little time analyzing the inner you — discovering in what situations you are the happiest, just exactly what turns you on. Socrates had a point when he said that the basis of wisdom is self-knowledge and from that awareness all other knowledge can be acquired. Surely it is impossible to understand anything until you understand yourself.

Self-Analysis Quiz

I've prepared a few questions which, if considered carefully, will give you more insights into your preferences and will help you in career evaluations. A space is provided for your answer to the left of the question.

_____ 1. Person- or thing-oriented? Are you happiest:

    (a) spending an evening with friends?

    (b) working alone sewing, knitting, building models or engaging in any other craft?

_____ 2. Do you find yourself:

    (a) believing in the pursuit of money as an end in itself?

    (b) an idealist who is seduced by "causes"?

_____ 3. Are you a person who:

    (a) works best under pressure and is happiest when faced with almost insurmountable demands?

    (b) enjoys a steady, quiet, predictable pace?

_____ 4. Are you usually the "life of the party," the person who initiates group activities?

    (a) Yes   (b) No

_____ 5. Are you happiest when you can be of service to others?

    (a) Yes   (b) No

_____ 6. Are you more comfortable when involved with:

    (a) measurable facts?

    (b) creative, abstract ideas?

_____ 7. Are you happiest when not confined to an office or lab? Do you like to work outdoors?

    (a) Yes   (b) No

_____ 8. Are you interested in travel — seeing the country, the world?

    (a) Yes   (b) No

AN ANALYSIS OF YOUR ANSWERS

1. If your answer was (a), you should work in a people-oriented field, i.e.,

Sales	Receptionist
Personnel	Hostess
Social Work	Public Relations
Teaching	Administration

If your answer was (b) (hobbies you engage in alone), you would probably be happier in a field *not* involved with one-to-one relationships, such as:

Lab Technician	Copyediting
Accounting	Science (Chemistry, Physics, Biology)
Drafting	
Bookkeeping	Math and Statistics

2. If your answer was (a), you would be happy in a profit-making business. Your choices include:

Investments and Banking	Insurance and Credit
Advertising and Sales Promotion	Manufacturing, Printing, etc.

If your answer was (b), you should try for a job in:

Social Service   Health Fields

Fund-Raising   Foundations*

3. If your answer was (a), you will find plenty of pressure in such fields as:

    1) Service businesses:

        Advertising   Public Relations

        Temporary   Employment
          Services   Agencies

        Interior   Sales
          Decorating

    2) Businesses involving deadlines:

        Newspapers   Book and Magazine
                       Publishing

        Tax Accountants   TV Producing

For those who chose (b), a quieter, steadier pace may be found in such fields as:

    Library Science   Copyediting

    Computer   The Sciences
      Programming   (Chemistry,
                      Biology, Physics)
    Math and
      Statistics

4. If you answered "yes," you probably are an extrovert and would be happiest in:

    Sales   Public Relations

    Advertising   Performing Arts

    Executive and
    Administrative Positions

*Don't forget that these fields also employ attorneys, writers, accountants, secretaries, executives.

5. If you answered "yes," you probably would be very successful in such fields as:

Therapy (Psychological, Speech, Occupational, Physical)	Nursing
	Social Work

6. If your answer was (a), you will be happiest in such fields as:

Research (Political, Historical, Market, Media, Financial, Consumer, etc.)	Sciences (Chemistry, Physics, Biology)
	Math and Statistics
	Accounting and Bookkeeping

Those who answered (b) should search for careers in:

Publishing	Films and Television
Advertising and Public Relations	Interior Decorating and Design

7. If you answered "yes," consider the following fields:

Athletic Instructor	Door-to-Door Sales
	Athletics
Landscape Architecture	Police Work

8. If you answered "yes," you might investigate the following fields:

Journalism	The Military
Sales	Diplomacy
Aviation	Flight Attendant

This short questionnaire is, of course, incomplete but it should give you some direction in your attempt to understand yourself. Careful and honest introspection is necessary, and once you discover what you *really* want, you will find such knowledge invaluable.

What Fields Are Open?

Employment agencies all over the country report that business is great. Personnel departments are still complaining of the difficulties in filling certain jobs. In many large cities real estate brokers are reporting shortages of available office space. All of these are signs of a healthier economy.

The recession will soon be a thing of the past, hence more and more jobs will become available. At the present time, there are many openings in the following fields:

Computer Science
(skyrocketing)

CRT operator
Data processing
Key punch
Programming
Research
Systems analyst
Technician

Design
(average to high competition)

Architecture
Commercial artists
Display
Fashion
Floral
Industrial
Interior
Landscaping
Urban planners

Driving
(average)

Bus
Chauffeur
Local merchandise delivery
Long-distance trucking
Taxi

Engineering
(booming)

Aerospace
Agricultural
Biomedical
Chemical
Civil
Electrical
Mining
Petroleum

Environmental Protection
(average to great)

Energy exploration
Forestry
Geology
Meteorology
Oceanography
Research and analysis
Sanitation
Urban renewal

Financial
(average)

Accountant
Actuary
Analyst
Banking
(manager, teller, credit counselor, investor)
Insurance
Marketing
Real estate
Stock broker

Law
(average)

Administrative
Government law specialist
Lawyer
Paralegal

Medical
(growing rapidly)

Administrative

Dentist

Dietician

Doctor
*(general practitioner or
hospital specialist)*

Electrocardiograph technician

Emergency medical technician

Lab technician

Nurse

Optometrist

Paramedical

Pharmacist

Radiologist

Research

Therapist
*(physical, occupational
or recreational)*

Office Help
(average)

Accounting clerk
Administrative assistant
Bookkeeper
Figure clerk
File clerk
Gal/Guy Friday
Office manager
Receptionist
Secretary
Typist

Publishing
(average)

Acquisitions
Copyediting
Editorial assistant
Production
Proofreading
Subsidiary rights
Writing

Sales
(average)

Canvassing
Marketing
Purchasing
Retailing
Travel

According to a 1981 survey by the Bureau of Labor Statistics, fields offering the most promise in the 1980s are:

Data Processing
Paralegal Services
Computer Technology
Food Preparation
Employment Interviewing
Architecture
Dentistry
Physical Therapy
Child Care Services
Veterinary Science
Travel Agencies
Health Care — particularly nurses' aides and orderlies

Where Do You Find Work? 8

Look around You

A job search, like charity, begins at home. Of all the various job sources, the most convenient — and at times, the best — are your relatives, friends and neighbors. Almost anyone you know may be able to furnish you with the lead you've been looking for. So, if you're on the job market, don't keep it quiet; part of your campaign is to let as many people as possible know that you are job hunting.

Don't be embarrassed about spreading the word. Your friends, too, have been in your position and know that any help is welcome. Were the positions reversed and a friend asked you for help, wouldn't you be eager to assist in any way you could?

Often people who are employed hear of job openings in their companies before the jobs are advertised or listed with employment agencies. Not only are they the first to know about the vacancies, but companies do tend to give preference in hiring to people recommended by their own employees rather than to a complete stranger. Often, at my agency, when following up one of our applicants, we have found out that the job went to a friend of an employee even though we knew our applicant was a perfect "fit" with both the job and the company.

Even though a "friend at court" is no guarantee of getting a job, it is far more likely that you will reach the interview stage if recommended by an employee of that company than would someone answering an ad or sent by an agency. In job hunting you always have to contend with human nature. An employer feels more secure about a prospect referred by someone he knows than about a complete stranger. Wouldn't you?

Now — if you are convinced of the foregoing and believe that someone you know is going to be instrumental in finding you a job, you are going to wonder if you shouldn't put off preparing a résumé until it's "needed." We agree. You shouldn't go to the trouble and expense of preparing a résumé until it *is* needed, and it is needed the moment you decide to look for work. If a friend or relative suggests your name to his company, it is almost certain that he or she will get back to you and say, "I've told them about you and they're interested, but first they want to see a résumé."

It is often a good idea to give the people you know copies of your résumé. It helps them in talking about you to people they think can help you, and in addition, they can speed up the decision process by handing in the résumé for you.

Classified Ads

Read the ads! There is a wealth of information in the classified columns of your newspaper. You may not find the job of your dreams (although you might), but you can learn much about the job market by going over the classified ads. You will see what kinds of jobs are open and can get an idea about salaries in the various fields. Through the ads, you have a means of testing whether the salary you're hoping for is in line with reality, or, for that matter, whether your job expectations are realistic. You can tell whether you are selling yourself short or aiming too high.

When searching the ads, consider all job titles. An opening for a bookkeeper, for example, may be listed under "Accounting"; an administrative assistant's position could be advertised as "Executive Secretary." Don't let the job titles mislead you; read the entire body of the ad. The duties required and the qualifications desired can give much more information about the job than can its title. The vocabulary of job hunting can overwhelm you with its confusion. An assistant to an editor might be advertised as "Editorial Assistant," "Secretary to the Editor," "Guy/Gal Friday," or even "Publishing Assistant."

Be careful not to ignore a good opportunity simply because the job title is not what you might have expected. Be sure to read the classified section carefully and respond to every ad that might be a "possible." Remember, too, that salaries are approximate. Very often jobs are filled at salaries higher or lower than those offered in the ads. Ultimately, salary depends upon the qualifications of the person selected. For this reason, it is advisable to answer all ads (with which your qualifications coincide to some degree) even if the salary offered is in the extreme lower limit of your range. A job listed at $15 thousand might be filled eventually at a salary of $18 thousand, or one advertised as "to $13 thousand" might only go to $11 thousand. In addition, a job listed at a salary less than you had anticipated could offer so much growth and opportunity that it might bear investigation.

Since you are looking for the best possible job, it is advisable to explore as many opportunities as possible, to present yourself at as many interviews as you can, and to learn as much about each job offered as you are able. Then, after careful consideration of each job with all of its opportunities, benefits, and ramifications, you accept the one that most closely resembles what you are looking for. (We will go into this in much greater detail towards the end of this book.)

Be sure to follow the directions given in each particular ad. If a phone number is listed and it is requested that you call for an appointment, do so; don't arrive without warning. Some job seekers think that an unannounced arrival shows great enthusiasm. It doesn't. What it does is waste both your and the interviewer's time, and creates hostility. If a box number is listed, reply by sending your résumé with a covering letter as discussed in Chapter 6.

Don't be discouraged if you don't get immediate results. At times, as much as three months can elapse before receiving a response to your résumé. Remember that job hunting is harder and more frustrating than working, but once you have had success in your search, the weeks, or even months of anxiety and anguish will be forgotten very quickly.

Private Employment Agencies

Anyone out job hunting should consider the services of the private employment agency. Their business consists of trying to find the right people for the jobs and the right jobs for the people. They might be able to offer you the help you need. The private agencies recruit and screen applicants for many different firms and, therefore, are in a position to introduce you to a number of prospective employers.

Therefore, going to an employment agency is equivalent to applying for a variety of job openings. The agency can describe every opening that it has listed which could be filled by a person with your qualifications and leave you the choice of which ones you want to investigate further. Effectively, the agency does your leg work for you and will keep you informed of new job openings as they arise. Most agencies expect and need résumés, and you should be prepared to give them several copies.

Private agencies charge a fee which may be paid by the job seeker or the employer or be divided between them. The fee is charged only in the event that the agency finds you a job that you are willing to accept. Be sure that you fully understand what the remuneration agreement is. If you are asked to sign a contract, ascertain precisely what you are committed to before you accept a job. Today it is more customary for the employer to pay the full fee, but many agencies still have jobs listed where the applicant must pay. Some employers may prefer to reimburse the employee for the fee after a certain length of employment. Don't feel embarrassed to ask the interviewer at the agency to clarify any questions about the contract. As with any other business arrangement, it is best to have a complete understanding of terms at the very beginning of your relationship with the agency.

Finding the appropriate agency is also a very important consideration on the job hunt. Most agencies specialize in certain fields or professions; so, be sure that the agencies you register with handle your skills or professional qualifications. If you are a graduate engineer, there is no point in registering with an agency that specializes in accountants and bookkeepers. Study the agencies' ads in the classified columns of the newspaper; the types of jobs they advertise will generally indicate their area of specialization.

Since employment agencies are completely involved in recruiting, they can be helpful in advice about current job trends and market conditions. Quite often, too, they are able to assume some of the functions of the trained guidance counselor. Since they are in continual touch with the job market, they are able to see that your particular skills may be appropriate to an industry that you had never considered worth investigating.

A few years ago, my agency interviewed a young man who was what is often called "over qualified." He had a Ph.D. in Romance Languages, was completely bilingual in Spanish and English, and had reading and writing ability in French and Italian. He did not want to teach and had followed up what he considered to be every lead for a person of his training — United Nations, foreign embassies and consulates, import-export firms, multi-national corporations, and so on. The offers he received, he had refused, since he felt the salaries were completely unrealistic. We agreed with him, but didn't feel we could do anything at the moment for him. His résumé was passed around the office and our law desk called one of her accounts which had a heavy international practice. Unfortunately the applicant needed a law degree to go with the bilingualism. Three days later, however, the law firm called back suggesting we contact an underwriter at a large marine insurance company. The outcome was that the applicant found a job at the managerial level and commensurate pay in a field that he had never considered.

For an agency to find a job in this manner — where an employer account unable to take an applicant suggests that the agency try to place him with another particular company — is not unusual. You have to consider your counselor at the agency as your ally. The agency wants to place you and it wants to place you in the best job available for you. That is its function and, if it wants to stay in business, it has to perform it.

State and Government Employment Agencies

Another fine source of job leads is the state or government employment agency. Unlike private, commercial agencies, government agencies charge no fee to either the job applicant or the employer. Their functions are supported by the government.

If you are serious about your job search, you should visit your local government employment office to avail yourself of its services. In addition to advising you of job openings in the immediate vicinity, the counselors at these agencies can also give you information on obtaining a government job.

Chamber of Commerce

Your Chamber of Commerce can be extremely helpful in your job search. It can supply you with a list of all of the companies in your area. Such a list would be excellent for your personal direct mail campaign. You might even learn from the Chamber of Commerce of actual job openings and which companies would be most interested in your skills and qualifications.

Government Jobs

Don't overlook the possibilities that government can offer. The U.S. government employs over 17 million Americans. One out of 6 employed persons serve either federal, state or local governments. The federal government employs 2.8 million, the state government employs 4 million, and local government over 8 million. U.S. government agencies hire 13,000–18,000 recent college grads a year. These statistics represent a significant portion of the work force and, therefore, a government position is an option which should be taken seriously.

The range of job offerings is tremendous. Doctors, attorneys, secretaries, clerks are employed by the government, as well as teachers, engineers, gardeners, and chauffeurs. Think of a job classification and rest assured that the government employs people in that category. Many people feel that the government jobs offer the most security (or *did* until the recent recession), the best health plans, the most liberal vacations, and the most extensive retirement plans.

The government, perhaps, is the only employer that is not interested in your résumé. Governmental positions have precise and inflexible educational and experiental requirements which must be met in order to *apply* for a given job. All that meeting these requirements entitles you to is the opportunity to take an examination for the job. The examination is both determinative and competitive. That is, you must achieve a certain grade in order to be eligible for the job, but the job will be offered first to the person who achieved the highest score on the test. Depending upon the job, the test may be written, practical, or physical. A sanitation engineer must be strong enough to lift a garbage pail, and a chauffeur must be able to drive, not merely know the traffic rules and the simple repair of a car.

Should you take a test for a government job and not score high enough to fill one of the immediately available openings, you may be eligible for subsequent openings. Usually, each "class" taking the examination retains its eligibility for a certain period of time, and during that time no additional examinations are given. Customarily, examinations are given every six months, every year, or every two or three years. As a rule, if you are still interested in a position when an examination occurs again, you must take the exam again to determine your eligibility.

Should you be interested in government employment, you have to be very methodical in seeking it out. You must find out what the offerings are that might be available immediately and in the future at every government level. There is no single office that takes care of federal, state, county, and municipal employment: each has to be applied for in its appropriate office.

On the municipal level, a call to your city or town hall will tell you where to go and whom to see. For county employment, another phone call will start the ball rolling. On the search for employment with your state government, you should check the phone book to see if there is an office of the State Civil Service Commission (or Personnel Board) near you. If not, you should write to the State Civil Service Commission requesting a list of current examinations and job openings.* You should also ask to be put on their regular mailing list. In this manner you will obtain continuous up-to-date information.

The main post office in your town will have some information on examinations and openings in the Federal Civil Service.** More complete information may be obtained from the nearest local of-

---

*See also *Barron's How to Prepare for Civil Service Examinations* (Clerks, Typists, Stenographers, and Other Office Positions).

**See also *Barron's How to Prepare for the Professional and Administrative Career Examination (PACE)*. This exam may be taken by those holding the bachelor's degree or having the equivalent in working and/or education/working experience.

fice of the Federal Civil Service Commission or from the main office in Washington, D.C. Again, you should request to be put on the regular mailing list. It is worth noting that U.S. government jobs are available abroad as well as within the United States.

If you are interested in government work, stay with it. Read all of the literature available — your local library is a fine source. Take all tests for which you are eligible. There are enormous opportunities in government, and it is likely that your perseverance will get you the job you want.

Temporary Services

Temporary services can be extremely useful. Not only are they a means of supporting yourself during your job campaign, but they can even help you in getting the kind of job you really want. They are especially of value to beginners, people in the intermediate level, and those returning to the job market after an absence.

Most job seekers tend to overlook this source. They feel that, as their goal is a *permanent* position, they have nothing to gain by taking temporary employment. On the surface this would appear logical, but it does not consider the fact that a temporary position is often the opening wedge of the perfect job opportunity. Quite often, my agency has found that while our permanent division is recruiting for a specific job, our temporary division has sent a "temp" to cover the position until it was filled. We have become accustomed to learning that the "temp" was hired on a permanent basis.

It makes sense. While temps are often hired to provide extra force during an occasional moment of surge in a company's work load or to fill in for a sick or vacationing employee, they are also called in to keep the work from piling up on a desk that has unexpectedly become vacant. While the original intention is to interview other people to fill the job, the temp is on the spot demonstrating a capability for the job. No longer an unknown applicant, the temp often will be hired ahead of a person replying to an ad offering the permanent position. Often, too, the temp being a proven worker, the salary offer will be higher than that listed in the "specs" for the permanent position.

We had interviewed a highly experienced copywriter who had lost his job because of a slow advertising market. As our permanent division had nothing to offer him at the time, he asked if our temporary division could find him something — *anything*. As he explained, he was basically a lazy person and felt that any length of time collecting unemployment insurance would be psychologically disastrous for him. He also preferred to work as an office temporary rather than be overqualified in a permanent position.

Our temporary division sent him to a major oil company as a typist. As the gesture wouldn't cost him anything, he took his résumé along and left it with personnel. After working a few weeks as a typist, he was hired for an editorial position on the company's house organ. This position was not even known to us, as the oil company hadn't even gotten around to listing it!

A young woman came to us a few years ago with aspirations of getting into the publishing field. She had no previous experience, having just graduated from college, and in addition, she was job hunting at a time when most publishing houses were cutting back on staff. Desperate for work, she took temporary assignments, going from one company to another working as a clerk/typist. While filling in at the offices of a professional engineering society, she was offered a job as editorial assistant in their publications department. She called us a short time ago asking us to recruit an editorial assistant for her; she had been promoted to a full editorial position. The most remarkable part of this incident is that if we had received a call for an editorial assistant from the engineering society, we never would have sent that woman. In our previous dealings with them, they had always insisted on some engineering background for employees in their publications department. This woman, however, being on the spot, was able to demonstrate that her other skills and her intelligence more than made up for the deficiency in her background.

In the job search it is always advisable to take any opportunity that lets you get your foot in the door and prove your capabilities. In addition to offering this, it also permits you to enlarge your list of contacts by meeting new people. It is not unusual for your supervisor on a temporary job, impressed by your work and learning that you are marking time until you can find a permanent position, to suggest possibilities and leads you wouldn't have found otherwise.

It is important, therefore, while working as a temp, to do the best job you can, and to let everyone you meet while working know that you're looking for a permanent position. You never know who will introduce you to your new employer; so, bring copies of your résumé with you and leave one or two with anyone who shows interest in helping you.

Another advantage of the temporary services is that they can be extremely helpful to beginners or to persons who are not yet sure where their interests lie. Temporary work lets you experiment, spending a few days in one industry, perhaps a week or so in an art gallery, or possibly a month with a non-profit organization. It is a way of seeing how each field works and helping you collect information necessary for a wise and considered career choice.

Working on temporary assignments brings no guarantee of a permanent job offer, but there is a guarantee that you'll meet a variety of people, be exposed to many different kinds of businesses, and experience various distinctive working conditions. Most important of all, you will be gaining additional experience — all of this while getting paid for it! By all means, consider temporary work while on your quest for a permanent job.

Volunteer Work

It may seem strange, but occasionally it can be profitable for you to work for nothing. Volunteer work, like temporary work, is a way of meeting people. As we cannot stress enough, the more people you meet, the greater the possibility that someone will be able to point you in the direction of your dream job. Further, volunteer work can give you the opportunity of improving skills that are not yet sufficiently developed for remunerative employment.

One of the unexpected delights about volunteer work is that you never know with whom you might be working. Some of those people you see answering the phones on educational television stations during fund-raising campaigns are very high-salaried executives of established companies. One of New York's leading industrial designers spends his Saturdays with three other volunteers at the sales desk of a New York museum. The wife of the owner of one of New York's finest French restaurants spends her Wednesday evenings in the company of ten to twelve other people — most of whom couldn't afford a meal in her husband's establishment — stuffing envelopes for a non-profit organization.

Not only can you meet people who might help you find a job, but at times the volunteer work itself can become a paid position. The woman who directs the display department of a large upstate New York museum first started with them ten years ago when it was only a *small* upstate New York museum. Growing nonprofit organizations often recruit new employees from the ranks of their volunteers.

Even if your volunteer work does not lead, directly or indirectly, to a job, it is a way of filling empty time and can also fill other voids in your life. You meet people who share interests similar to your own, as well as people who range across a far wider social and economic scale than you would normally meet. Even if you ignore the fact that you are doing a "good deed," it is not time wasted.

Direct Mail Campaign

You cannot claim to have done all that is possible to find work if you have not conducted a direct mail campaign. Obviously, your résumé will be an integral part of this campaign; so, once you have prepared the best possible résumé, you are ready to start.

With your résumé ready, your next task is to compile a list of possible employers. If you want to work where you live or within commuting distance of your home town, the Yellow Pages of your telephone directory is one of your best possible sources. If you are willing to relocate, the reference librarian at your local library will be an excellent source of information for you. She can refer you to the books you need to compile your list. As a rule, you are not allowed to withdraw these books, but will have to prepare your list in the library's reference room. Since you will probably find you need other information as you go along, this is not great inconvenience.

The list should not be too long. You don't want to feel that you have involved yourself in an interminable project. Bear in mind that every company on the list is going to be sent a covering letter with your résumé. This requires your determining the name and title of the person you plan to write to. Such reference books as Standard and Poor's can give you this information. Again, the reference librarian can help you.

If you are willing to relocate, do not hesitate to write to companies at a distance from your home. Most companies, when faced by a really "hot" applicant, will either send someone to interview the applicant or pay for the applicant's trip to their main offices. If you are willing to relocate, you should so state on your résumé; otherwise, the company is apt to assume that you are looking for an opening in their office near your home.

Your covering letter should be brief and written in a conversational, but not "cute," tone. Simply say that you are enclosing your résumé and would like to be considered for a position in that company. Also include a short statement indicating why you feel your qualifications will interest the firm. As you are enclosing a résumé which gives a detailed description of your talents and skills, there is no need to be too verbose in your covering letter.

The letter should never exceed four paragraphs. Your final paragraph should state that you will call in a few days hoping to arrange for an interview. *Don't wait for them to call.* The closer you come to personal contact, the closer you are to a job offer.

I cannot overemphasize the need to type *individually* every covering letter. You may reproduce your résumé; never your letter. The letter should have the format of a standard business letter with sufficient margin all around to present an attractive appearance. Don't forget that it is your first introduction to a prospective employer.

Following Through

Keeping a Record

Keep a record of each résumé sent and note the dates of your calls and interviews. Also indicate the results of each call and interview, and remember your follow-up letters. Don't leave anything to your memory; maintain a written record.

The simplest way of maintaining a record of your direct mail campaign is to make a carbon copy of each covering letter as you type it. On the bottom of the carbon, you can note date and result of your phone call, date of interview, result of interview, and follow-up note. These can be kept in a file folder with a separate sheet — or calendar page — with dates and times of interviews noted. It would be disastrous to set up two interviews for the same time.

A second system is to set up a large sheet of paper with column headings across the top of the sheet. The information, of course, would be the same as that maintained by using carbon copies. Below is the suggested heading for each column. The headings would be separated by lines drawn vertically down the full length of the sheet, and horizontal lines would be drawn, each about two inches below the other, to separate the entries for each company written. I suggest the following headings:

Résumé Mailing	Follow-Up Phone Call	Interview	Thank-You Letter	Job Offer	Confirmation or "No Thank You, But" Letter
Name	Date	Date	Date	Yes	Date
Title	Results	Time		No	Letter Type
Company		Interviewer			
Address		Results			
Date Sent					

Note that record-keeping sheets of this type have been provided on pages 263 through 266 for your convenience.

The third system involves the use of 4″ × 6″ index cards. Again the information would be the same as the other systems. Below is a sample layout for the card:

Mr. Richard Rowe   Mailed 3/22/76
Chief Draftsman
Systems, Inc.
424 Park Place
Buford, Pa. 21370

Phone Call: _____
                                        (indicate date)

(Note results) _____

Interview: _____
                             (indicate date, time, and interviewer)

(Note results) _____

Thank-You Letter _____
                                        (indicate date)

Job Offer _____

Confirmation *or* "No Thank You, But" Letter _____
                                               (indicate date and letter type)

This system is best for a very large mailing. I suggest that you have the index cards printed up cheaply rather than trying to type them yourself.

A direct mail campaign is not an inexpensive way of looking for work, but no way really is. Direct mail involves an expenditure of money — for reproduction of résumés, envelopes, postage, and phone calls — and time. But any other method involves as much time. The difference is that the direct mail time is spent in the comfort of your home instead of on buses, on the pavement, and in waiting rooms. If you are pounding the pavements looking for work, you also have expenses for car fare, lunches, and the continual cups of coffee. I point this out mainly to remind you that the job hunt is going to cost you regardless of how you do it. You've got to spend in order to earn.

KEEPING A RECORD

Résumé Mailing

Name _____

Title _____

Company _____

Address _____

_____

Date Sent _____

Follow-Up Phone Call

Date _____

Results _____

_____

_____

Interview

Date _____

Time _____

Interviewer _____

_____

Results _____

Thank-You Letter

Date _____

_____

Job Offer

Yes _____

No _____

Confirmation or "No Thank You, But" Letter

Date _____

Letter Type _____

Résumé Mailing

Name _____

Title _____

Company _____

Address _____

_____

Date Sent _____

Follow-Up Phone Call

Date _____

Results _____

_____

_____

Interview

Date _____

Time _____

Interviewer _____

_____

Results _____

Thank-You Letter

Date _____

_____

Job Offer

Yes _____

No _____

Confirmation or "No Thank You, But" Letter

Date _____

Letter Type _____

Résumé Mailing

Name _____

Title _____

Company _____

Address _____
_____

Date Sent _____

Follow-Up Phone Call

Date _____

Results _____

Interview

Date _____

Time _____

Interviewer _____
_____

Results _____

Thank-You Letter

Date _____
_____

Job Offer

Yes _____

No _____

Confirmation or "No Thank You, But" Letter

Date _____

Letter Type _____
_____

Résumé Mailing

Name _____

Title _____

Company _____

Address _____
_____

Date Sent _____

Follow-Up Phone Call

Date _____

Results _____

Interview

Date _____

Time _____

Interviewer _____
_____

Results _____

Thank-You Letter

Date _____
_____

Job Offer

Yes _____

No _____

Confirmation or "No Thank You, But" Letter

Date _____

Letter Type _____
_____

KEEPING A RECORD

Résumé Mailing

Name _____

Title _____

Company _____

Address _____

Date Sent _____

Follow-Up Phone Call

Date _____

Results _____

Interview

Date _____

Time _____

Interviewer _____

Results _____

Thank-You Letter

Date _____

Job Offer

Yes _____

No _____

Confirmation or "No Thank You, But" Letter

Date _____

Letter Type _____

Résumé Mailing

Name _____

Title _____

Company _____

Address _____

Date Sent _____

Follow-Up Phone Call

Date _____

Results _____

Interview

Date _____

Time _____

Interviewer _____

Results _____

Thank-You Letter

Date _____

Job Offer

Yes _____

No _____

Confirmation or "No Thank You, But" Letter

Date _____

Letter Type _____

KEEPING A RECORD

Résumé Mailing

Name _____

Title _____

Company _____

Address _____
_____

Date Sent _____

Follow-Up Phone Call

Date _____

Results _____
_____
_____

Interview

Date _____

Time _____

Interviewer _____

Results _____
_____

Thank-You Letter

Date _____

Job Offer

Yes _____

No _____

Confirmation or "No Thank You, But" Letter

Date _____

Letter Type _____

Résumé Mailing

Name _____

Title _____

Company _____

Address _____
_____

Date Sent _____

Follow-Up Phone Call

Date _____

Results _____
_____
_____

Interview

Date _____

Time _____

Interviewer _____

Results _____
_____

Thank-You Letter

Date _____

Job Offer

Yes _____

No _____

Confirmation or "No Thank You, But" Letter

Date _____

Letter Type _____

The Interview

The initial interview should not be viewed with alarm nor with fear and trembling. (There — I've said it. And you, believing every word I've written, suddenly wonder whether I know what I'm talking about. Trust me — I do!) If you find yourself shaking at the prospect of an interview, you had better realize that you have plenty of company. The tens of thousands of people my agency has sent out on interviews all had one feature in common: they had completely unrealistic fears about being interviewed and these fears stemmed from their being preoccupied with their weaknesses rather than their strengths.

Trust me. If you examine the interviewing process realistically, you will see that it loses much of its terror. It is not the ladder up to the guillotine, nor is it an inquisitorial process designed to bring you to your knees admitting to your worthlessness. It is nothing more than a meeting arranged to amplify the material contained in your résumé and to inform you in more detail of the various facets of the job in question. Never forget that the interview is bilateral.

The company that is interviewing you is just as interested in selling itself to you as you are in selling yourself to the company. Your résumé has already done most of the job of selling you. If it hadn't, you wouldn't be at an interview. Very often, after a few questions to clarify or expand upon the details in your résumé, you suddenly find that the interviewer is no longer talking about you, but is telling you of the tremendous advantages of working for that company. You may not realize something that is very clear to me from my perspective — that many a company has lost an applicant it wanted badly, because the interviewer at one of its competitors described a much more attractive working environment.

You are not present at the interview because the company wants to do its part to lower the unemployment rate. Your presence is a result of a personnel director or other representative feeling that the firm's interests can be served by hiring you. As a rule, they have, or soon will have, an opening to be filled and are trying to get the best qualified person they can to fill it. The information they have through your résumé has indicated that you *are* qualified; through the interview, they are trying to determine if you are the *best* qualified.

With this in mind — that the company *is* interested in you — your effort must be directed toward convincing them that *their* best interest lies in hiring *you*. Through your manner you have to indicate that you are not only the best qualified among the interviewees, but that you have assets and abilities that can't display themselves in a résumé. The amplification that the interviewer often seeks are those intangibles which will ultimately decide whether you and the firm are suitable for one another.

This may seem a strange basis for hiring, but it usually is the decisive factor. When my agency sends a well-qualified applicant out on an interview, it is our practice, if the applicant is not hired, to call the account to find out why they were not satisfied. We do this in order to learn if there were "holes" in the job specifications we were given, or if the applicant was rejected as a result of details not included in the résumé. (We are trying to better our service both to the applicant and to the account — to the account, the employer, by not sending unqualified people; to the applicant-client, by not setting up interviews which are doomed beforehand.) On occasions we find that there are concrete reasons for the rejection, but it is more common for us to be told, ". . . not our kind of person," or ". . . wasn't an X Company employee," or ". . . wouldn't be happy with us." We have learned that it is futile to try to get more information in these cases. It isn't that the personnel people don't want to tell us; they themselves can't explain what they *feel* is wrong.

It is difficult to determine what is wrong when the people making the decisions don't know themselves. However, employment agencies have become fairly good at predicting which applicants are going to get hired and which are not going to be, for the intangibles affect all of us as well. At my agency, we have come to the conclusion that the three most important intangibles are enthusiasm, sincerity, and honesty.

By enthusiasm, we do not mean a bubbling, ingenuous exuberance. On the other hand, we do not mean — very definitely — a "cool." Any attempt to be "cool" will be interpreted as boredom, apathy, or antagonism on your part, and such attitudes inevitably lead to a rapid, and unsatisfactory, termination of the interview. Enthusiasm can be shown by manifesting an interest in the job under consideration, in the company offering the job, or even in the interviewing process itself. A simple way of showing interest is to do a little research on the company before the interview. This invariably creates a favorable impression. Furthermore, if the information you obtain on the firm impresses *you* favorably, it has a tendency to "psych you up," to make you *want* to get that particular job, and that, in itself, will come out as enthusiasm as you are interviewed.

Not only should you avoid trying to be "cool," but you should shun assuming any *persona* that is not your own, as well as any other semblance of role-playing. There are two reasons for this. First of all, few of us have sufficient acting ability to permit us to continue in a role for any length of time, and we would rapidly give ourselves away. Secondly, no amount of research is going to show you what sort of a person, apart from your qualifications as a worker, the company is interested in. Even if there is a readily identifiable IBM or Random House or Young and Rubicam image, you have no way of knowing if you are not the first person to be interviewed after top management has decided that the firm is going to have to change its public image.

Be yourself! Walking into an interview with this intention will be the first step toward losing the interview "jitters." Knowing that you will be hired for your qualifications and for your personality, *just as they are*, goes a long way toward making you appear an interested and sincere prospect.

It is wise to reread your résumé before each interview. Going over your background in this way will help you present yourself as a well-organized person with a calm and positive manner. It is also a means of helping you recall facts, through association, which are not on the résumé, but which will probably come up in the interview. These facts will be found quite often on an application that you may be asked to fill out prior to the interview. (See the sample on pages 270 and 271). These facts will probably include such data as previous salaries, names of supervisors in your earlier jobs, and reasons for leaving former (or present) employment. As the interviewers often repeat questions already answered on your résumé or in the application, it is best if no appearance of confusion exists on your part.

This is also one of the prime reasons for being completely honest in the interview. If you depart from the truth in either your résumé or on the job application, you are putting an additional load on your memory and this will serve only to increase your apprehension. The interviewer expects some nervousness on your part and usually will try to help dispel it. However, if your nervousness increases as the interview continues, this can be interpreted as an indication that you are afraid of being found out in a lie. This is the one intolerable action in the eyes of any employer.

In a sense, your employment is an inarticulated contract between you and the company. There is a mutual benefit which both parties agree to after assessing the facts available to them. Either party would be justified in cancelling the unspoken contract if the other party had falsified any of the information. If you accepted a job at a low salary scale as a result of a promise of a sizable increase after three months' employment, you would feel that you had been treated unfairly if you were not accorded the raise when the time arrived. And your employer is equally justified in cancelling the contract if you had been hired as a result of false information.

It is not merely a matter of morality. Hiring and "breaking in" a new employee is an expensive process for a company. In addition to the clerical costs involved in setting up a new personnel file, adding to the insurance roster, setting up payroll cards, etc., there is also the fact that many offices feel that few employees can *earn* their salaries until having worked three months. One of the functions of the personnel department of any company is the avoidance of any such *unnecessary* expense. Hence, even the suspicion of a lie can keep you from being hired. For that reason it is best to be direct, candid, and honest in all your replies.

XYZ Co.
EMPLOYMENT APPLICATION

NEW YORK LAW PROHIBITS DISCRIMINATION
BECAUSE OF RACE, CREED, COLOR, NATIONAL ORIGIN,
SEX, AGE, OR DISABILITY.

INSTRUCTIONS:
PLEASE COMPLETE THIS APPLICATION FULLY AND ACCURATELY. ANSWERS SHOULD
BE PRINTED OR TYPEWRITTEN. ANY ADDITIONAL INFORMATION YOU WISH
TO SUBMIT MAY BE ATTACHED.

DATE OF APPLICATION	DATE AVAILABLE
POSITION DESIRED	SALARY DESIRED
HOW WERE YOU REFERRED TO XYZ Co. ?	

PERSONAL DATA

NAME IN FULL

MAILING ADDRESS

Zip Code

TELEPHONE

SOCIAL SECURITY NUMBER

U.S. CITIZEN ☐ YES ☐ NO

AVAILABLE FOR OVERTIME ☐ YES ☐ NO

TIME LOST THROUGH ILLNESS IN PAST TWO YEARS

NATURE OF ILLNESS

IN CASE OF EMERGENCY, PLEASE NOTIFY

NAME

ADDRESS

TELEPHONE
HOME: BUSINESS

EDUCATION

SCHOOL	ADDRESS	FROM	TO	MAJOR COURSE	CLASS RANK / GPA	DEGREE
HIGH SCHOOL						
COLLEGE/UNIVERSITY						
BUSINESS/TECHNICAL						
GRADUATE						
OTHER						

EXTRACURRICULAR ACTIVITIES
(OMIT THOSE THAT INDICATE RACE, CREED, COLOR, NATIONAL ORIGIN, SEX, AGE, OR DISABILITY)

ACADEMIC HONORS

FOREIGN LANGUAGES

MILITARY RECORD

MILITARY STATUS	MILITARY DUTIES
BRANCH OF MILITARY SERVICE RANK	
ACTIVE DUTY FROM: TO:	

REFERENCES (DO NOT INCLUDE RELATIVES OR EMPLOYERS)

NAME	ADDRESS	OCCUPATION
NAME	ADDRESS	OCCUPATION
NAME	ADDRESS	OCCUPATION

AN EQUAL OPPORTUNITY EMPLOYER   M/F

PREVIOUS EMPLOYMENT (MOST RECENT FIRST)

NAME OF EMPLOYER	POSITION
FULL ADDRESS	JOB DESCRIPTION
NAME OF IMMEDIATE SUPERVISOR	DATE STARTED / DATE LEFT
INITIAL SALARY / FINAL SALARY	REASON FOR LEAVING

NAME OF EMPLOYER	POSITION
FULL ADDRESS	JOB DESCRIPTION
NAME OF IMMEDIATE SUPERVISOR	DATE STARTED / DATE LEFT
INITIAL SALARY / FINAL SALARY	REASON FOR LEAVING

NAME OF EMPLOYER	POSITION
FULL ADDRESS	JOB DESCRIPTION
NAME OF IMMEDIATE SUPERVISOR	DATE STARTED / DATE LEFT
INITIAL SALARY / FINAL SALARY	REASON FOR LEAVING

NAME OF EMPLOYER	POSITION
FULL ADDRESS	JOB DESCRIPTION
NAME OF IMMEDIATE SUPERVISOR	DATE STARTED / DATE LEFT
INITIAL SALARY / FINAL SALARY	REASON FOR LEAVING

STENOGRAPHIC SPEED WPM	TYPING SPEED WPM	BUSINESS MACHINES OPERATED

I hereby affirm that my answers to the foregoing questions are true and correct. I understand that any misrepresentation of facts on this application constitutes sufficient cause for dismissal and that classification as a regular employee depends upon satisfactory performance during a three-month probationary period. I hereby grant XYZ Co. permission to verify any information presented on this application and further agree to submit to a medical examination by a physician designated by XYZ Co. if I am considered for employment.

SIGNATURE

DATE

FOR EMPLOYEE RELATIONS USE ONLY

POSITION TITLE	SALARY GRADE	SALARY	EMPLOYEE NUMBER
DEPARTMENT	STARTING DATE	ENTRY DATE	

☐ EXEMPT ☐ ADDITION

☐ NONEXEMPT ☐ REPLACEMENT FOR _____

HIRED BY

Many people, for instance, feel that they should exaggerate their previous salaries. Perhaps they feel that they are very well qualified for the $15 thousand-a-year job, but their previous salary being only $10 thousand will count against them; so, they put a little white lie on the application. Yet that may be one of the details that personnel will check when calling your previous employer. It is far better to be truthful.

It is possible that your previous employer was known through the industry for underpaying employees. It could also be obvious from your résumé that, as your skills and duties with that company increased over the years, your salary was not increased commensurately. If you do feel that the disparity between your previous salary and the one you are seeking is great, it is far better to explain that the low pay was one of the reasons you left that job.

Another of the inevitable questions on résumés concerns your reasons for leaving previous employment. Here again the undistorted truth is the only answer. Even if you were dismissed for incompetence, it is wise to say so. It can be very clear to the interviewer, on the basis of your résumé, that you never should have been given the previous job, that you were clearly underqualified for the position. It could be clear that not you, but the person who hired you, was to blame. Your honesty and candor would bring this out, in all likelihood.

Keep in mind that your résumé has preceded you and that much of the information that will be elicited in the interview is already implicit in your résumé. Personnel people are accustomed to reading between the lines and part of the clarification process in the interview consists of the interviewer verifying data of which he is almost sure. It is very improbable that the truth will be a complete surprise to the interviewer. So — stop worrying.

Also you must remember that anything can happen *once*. Interviewers start wondering when the unusual happens more than once. It can be accepted that you were fired from one job because your immediate superior ignored Satchel Paige's advice and looked over his shoulder — and saw you gaining on him. People have been fired because their superiors were afraid of the competition. And personnel people know this. *You* become the problem when you give this as the reason for having lost five jobs in two years.

Because anything can happen once, it is possible that you *are* concerned about the reference you would get from a previous employer. This is simply handled. Most personnel people ask if you would mind having any of your former employers called for references. In the event that you are worried about what one of them might say about you, merely tell the interviewer that you would prefer that one of them not be phoned. Then, tell the interviewer your reason for believing that you would get an unsatisfactory reference from that company. Once you have brought the matter to light, few personnel people would call to see if there was more to the story than you had divulged. Your candor in this situation serves a double purpose. First, it presents you as a person who is not only straightforward, but realistic as well. Second, it gives you one less thing to worry about when the interview is over. You don't have the unpleasantness in that previous job lurking in the shadows, ready to spring into the light; it is already in the open.

Even if you don't get the job, you must not dismiss the interview as time wasted. If you are a neophyte on the job market, at least you have experienced an interview and found out that it was not as terrifying as you had anticipated. You probably did make a good impression even if your qualifications were not quite what the company wanted. It is also likely that your résumé will be filed and you may be considered for another opening in the near future. This last is a very common occurrence; at my agency we often get calls asking if one of the applicants we had sent to an account months ago was still available for work.

Your appearance when you present yourself at any interview will affect its outcome. Appearance means not only the way you are dressed — which we will talk about shortly — but also the way you communicate non-verbally. You will never have to tell the interviewer that you are nervous in so many words; you will show that clearly by a number of gestures and movements. The nervousness will be understood. The problem will be in restraining those gestures and expressions that show boredom or hostility. While difficult to control, they can be suppressed if you will make an extremely conscious attempt to concentrate on the interviewer's words, even to the extent of subvocally repeating to yourself everything that is said. This concentration has a tendency to set up "interference" with the emotional connotation the words might have for you.

Another factor to consider is your actual physical appearance. Overdressing is as great an error as underdressing. The simplest rule to follow is to dress in the same way as you would expect to dress at work if you got the job. With very few exceptions, this means a suit, or sports jacket and trousers for men, and a dress or sweater (or blouse) and skirt or slacks for women. Your clothes should be neat and clean, and your hair should be so as well. Remember also that you are going to be interviewed by a human being with all of the quirks and prejudices of the species. That means that you do not want to engender instant antagonism by wearing a political button or insignia, or any indication of your views on any controversial subject. We are not suggesting that you have no right to your views, but merely recommending a platform other than a job interview for broadcasting those views.

DO'S AND DON'TS

There is much else we could tell you, but we feel that if you are intelligent enough to work, you are intelligent enough to know that you shouldn't pick your teeth or clean your fingernails at an interview. Advice of that kind you don't need. Below is a simplified list of the do's and don'ts of the interview.

- DON'T arrange for more than one interview in a morning or afternoon.

- DO be prompt at the appointed time. If for any reason you are delayed, phone and reschedule the interview as soon as you can.

- DO fill out application forms in their entirety even if you are asked for information already on your résumé.

- DO try to appear poised and alert. Make sure your clothing is comfortable, and try to seat yourself comfortably without sprawling.

- DON'T try to interview the interviewer. Trying to dominate the interview may give you a feeling of self-assurance, but it won't get you the job.

- DO ask questions. If there are aspects of the job that are not clear to you, ask. Whether your questions concern duties or benefits, you have a right to know.

- DON'T ask at the first opportunity what the paid holidays and vacations are. You don't want to give the impression that your prime interest is in how little work you will be doing.

- DON'T burden yourself with props. The initial interview is not the place for college credentials, letters of reference, work portfolios, and such, unless you are told to bring them.

- DO be polite at all times. Should the interviewer do anything to provoke your hostility, keep it under wraps until you get out.

- DON'T hide. Some people try to hide their nervousness by hiding parts of themselves. Such mannerisms as covering the mouth while talking or wearing sunglasses indoors are attempts at hiding.

- DON'T be vague. Your answers to all questions should be clear and definite. "I don't know" is often a very good answer to a question.

- DO know what you want. If the interviewer asks, "What kind of work would you like to do for us?" give a concrete answer. "I don't know; I'll do anything," gives the impression that there is nothing you can do.

- DON'T get downhearted. The failure to get a job from an interview doesn't mean that *you* are a failure. There are other jobs and other interviews.

- DO phone back after the interview. You may get the offer at the interview, or it may not come until later. One week after the interview, phone back and ask if you are still "at bat." Keep phoning until you get a definite answer.

A Postscript on Testing

Some companies today base their hiring decisions on skill, aptitude, intelligence, and personality tests. I will say at the outset that I, personally, think that all such tests are sheer nonsense. I am supported by large numbers of psychiatrists and psychologists in my belief. I am also opposed by a large number — most of whom earn their living by administering, interpreting, or designing such tests and of whom it may be argued that their opinion is biased.

This is not the place, however, to argue the advantages and disadvantages, or the merits and demerits of testing. They are a fact of life that you may encounter in searching for a job. The best way of handling them is to take them, and to take them in your stride.

If you have the skills, a test of your skills presents no problem. If you have ten solid years of experience as a journalist, an aptitude test that shows a deficiency in verbal ability is not likely to affect your employment. An intelligence test is something that may wind up in your personnel folder, but will have little effect on your career. This leaves the personality test.

The personality test can create problems both in your being hired and in your future career at that company. Without a doubt the personality test is the most dubious test of all, but it is the one that the "true believers" believe in the most. There are serious doubts about the legality of such tests, as they do ask extremely personal questions that often have little bearing upon the job in question. Many of the questions bear upon the religious beliefs or sexual attitudes of the testee and often fail to recognize that a test designed thirty years ago may not reflect today's norms. However, until the issue of legality is settled, my advice is to take the test as best you can, keeping in mind two things.

First, beware of all absolute questions that are to be answered with a "true or false" or a "yes or no." You have to consider how a "normal" person would answer. If the question is "Do you *ever* have sexual fantasies?" since most people do at one time or another, the answer is yes. But be careful of something like "Do you *often* have hostile feelings toward your parents?" Read all such questions very carefully, and watch those qualifying adverbs.

Second, keep your eyes open for the same question couched in different words. The designers of the tests expect people to try to "beat" them, and asking the same question in another form is one of the controls. For example, in a "yes or no" section of such a test, the question, "Do you ever have sexual fantasies?" might appear. Then, later, in a multiple choice section would appear the question, "How often do you have sexual fantasies?" with a choice of answers among "never — rarely — occasionally — frequently — constantly." A person who might not want to admit to "ever" having such fantasies might be willing, so runs the theory of the test, to answer "rarely" or even "occasionally."

There are books purporting to coach you in preparation for such tests. Our view is that a book which claims to prepare you for a mathematical ability test when math has always been your weakest subject, or for a mechanical aptitude test when you've never been able to get a cap off a child-proof bottle, is claiming to be able to accomplish the impossible. However, should you really think that one of them might help you, we suggest you look at it in your public library before buying it.

We've already discussed in detail how important a good résumé is, how to go about your job hunt, how to survive an interview, and how to follow up. Aside from phone calls, there are other methods of follow-up that will give you a good chance of getting the job.

Remember your competition. The company's personnel officer is considering other candidates for the open position as well as you. And, sometimes, it's really a toss-up. A follow-up letter can provide that extra push to get you in the company's door.

THE MAGIC POWER OF ENTHUSIASM

A simple explanation of how a follow-up letter can help you in competing for a job is that it provides the magic power of enthusiasm. Employment counselors usually agree that the most enthusiastic person gets the job in a toss-up. So why not provide the enthusiasm? It can only help.

IT PAYS TO SAY "THANK YOU"

The best way to follow up is to say "Thank you." You may want to say it to the person who told you about a job to let the person know that you appreciate the effort; or you may want to thank the interviewer, letting him or her know of your enthusiasm. The letter will keep your image fresh in the person's mind. And that's definitely a plus!

CONFIRMATION COURTESY

Even "after the fact," it pays to follow up. For example, you've been offered a job, and have accepted it. But you are presently working and have just given your employer two weeks' notice. A simple confirmation, accepting the job and thanking the person who's hiring you, will reassure your immediate supervisor-to-be that he or she has made the right decision; it may also assure you of a warmer reception two weeks hence when you show up for the first day on the job.

The confirmation should be simply written. Just confirm the fact that you have accepted the job, tell how happy you are to have it, and confirm the date on which you will report to start the job.

"NO THANK YOU, BUT . . ."

You have been offered a job, but for one reason or another you have refused it. It's an awkward situation that can be made smoother by a follow-up letter, especially if you are interested in working for the company, perhaps at some future time, or maybe in some other capacity that you have decided would better suit you.

Just let them know why you're refusing. Maybe you have accepted another job, but are unsure that it will work out satisfactorily. Then, letting them know will be a way of keeping your options open. If the company was interested enough in you to offer you a job at that time, it is quite possible that they will be happy to consider you for a job at some future time, providing the situation is mutually satisfactory. In other words, you are saying, "No thank you, but . . .," and who knows when your letter might pay off in the future. It's apt to make a good impression for your courtesy alone. Companies like to think they are worth your time and effort, especially when they have extended any courtesies to you. And, of course, they are worth it!

On the following pages are sample letters to illustrate what kind of letters we recommend. They are only suggestions, and your particular situation, plus your ingenuity, will dictate exactly what type of letter to write.

Sample Follow-up Notes

MODEL FOLLOW-UP NOTE CONFIRMING REFUSAL OF JOB OFFER,
BUT LEAVING OPTIONS OPEN

May 7, 1978

Mr. Richard Trump
Director of Social Work
Rockland Hospital
Rockland, Connecticut   06013

Dear Mr. Trump:

I regret that your job offer came a day too late. Just yesterday, I accepted a job as a social worker for another hospital. I am really sorry because I was impressed with your institution and probably would have fit in very well.

As I am not at all sure how my new job is going to work out, would you please be kind enough to keep my application on file, and contact me if there is another opening in the next few months?

Thank you for your offer, and again, I am sorry I have to refuse it.

Sincerely,

Anne Paulson

September 22, 1978

Ms. Joanna Crosley
Marketing Director
The Johnson Crumpf Company
1435 Commonwealth Avenue
Boston, Massachusetts 02117

Dear Ms. Crosley:

I am delighted to confirm my acceptance of the job as Senior Marketing Analyst. As you already know, I am not going to report for another two weeks. But I have just given my present firm two weeks' notice, and will report to you on October 4th.

Let me reiterate how pleased I am at getting this job. I was hoping that I would, as I feel that it is the perfect job for me and I know that I will fit into your company well.

Until October 4th, I am

Sincerely,

Barton Rockwood

April 12, 1978

Mr. David Jones
Public Relations Director
Smith & Krantz, Inc.
54 Alameda Street
Oakland, California 94610

Dear Mr. Jones:

I just wanted to write to tell you how pleased I was to meet with you last Thursday. Thank you for considering me for the position as your assistant. The job is just what I am looking for, and I think that I would be able to fit into your company very well.

Looking forward to hearing from you soon, I am

Sincerely,

Charles Brockton

March 31, 1979

Miss Sandra Morrisey
98 Auburn Street
Brookline, Massachusetts 02145

Dear Sandra:

 Thank you for telling me about the job as a Research Assistant with the Barkley Media Research Corporation. I have already interviewed with Jonathan Barkley, Jr., and I am glad to say that he seemed impressed with me and that the job is just what I am looking for.

 Mr. Barkley will be in touch with me next week with regard to my job application and my fingers are crossed in hopes of my getting the job.

 In any case, I want to thank you for taking the time to provide me with this information about a valuable job opportunity. I really appreciate it.

 Regards to your family, especially your sister, Alice, in Maine.

Sincerely,

Joan Smithers

Which Job Do I Take?

You've spent weeks on the hunt and you've bagged your quarry: two or three job offers. Now you have a new problem: your thoughts change from "How do I get the job I want?" to "Which one shall I accept?" What? You think that's an easy decision and that you'd take the job that offers the most money? Well, maybe yes, and maybe no. There's more to be considered than just money.

Say you're a recent college graduate and you never worked full-time before. You've come to a large metropolis because you know that's where your future lies. You don't know *anybody*. After weeks of searching you have had two job offers. In one, the higher paid of the two, you will be working in a small office with one or two other people; in the other, with five percent less pay, you'll be a member of a large staff and will have the opportunity to meet lots of people.

Since you've come to the city to start a whole new life, you must consider that a job that offers an opportunity to expand your social life might offer something as valuable as money. That is one of the many intangibles you must consider in the job selection process. Here are some others:

Some companies provide training programs; others are willing to pay part (or all) of the costs of specialized university courses for you to add to your skills and knowledge. How valuable is that? What is it worth? What will that additional education be worth in the future? This is another area to consider.

The geographical location of a job should influence your decision. If it would require you to relocate, should you? Have you thought about the cost of living in a different city? Remember, to judge the worth of your salary properly, it must be compared to the cost of living. What about cultural activities in the new city? And how important are they to you?

Even without relocation, you must consider the location of your job. Perhaps you are one of those people who seeks some diversion during the lunch hour — visiting a museum or doing some shopping. A job in the boondocks offering a few dollars more than one close to a cultural or shopping area might not interest you then. One requiring fifteen minutes' travel — a short walk from your home — could be preferable to another with a higher salary and an hour's bus or subway ride away. Often, a slight difference in salary is more than eaten up by transportation costs. Besides, time going to and from work is not exactly leisure time!

Be sure in making your decision that you consider the importance of being happy with your new job. My agency advises entry-level job seekers to take the job they instinctively feel "good" about. We've found that being happy in a job almost guarantees better job performance and hence promotion. We've also found that most companies promote from within and will always consider their staff members for each new job opportunity. Our philosophy is "Proximity is the mother of opportunity," and, therefore, the "wrong job in the right company" often or usually becomes the "right job in the right company."

A beginner should also consider possibilities in job hunting. Your first job should be considered as a place to learn, to get experience, and to prove yourself.

If you consider everything in your life as a growing experience and give it the best you have, you'll be bringing the ingredient of success to any job you take.

The many intangibles in selecting which job offer to take also apply to every job seeker.

For example, is there a company cafeteria? Many companies have them and offer good, nutritious food to their employees at low cost. Considering that, in many instances, a full meal at the company cafeteria will cost less than a hamburger and beverage at a luncheonette or fast-food counter, you would be able to save. How important would the advantages of this be in terms of economics and convenience? Certainly worth thinking about!

The health plan offered is another important factor. Young people very often tend to disregard a firm's hospital and major medical plans — they even consider themselves both indestructible and immortal! But anyone, of any age, can suddenly find himself or herself confronted with a stay in the hospital, resulting in large medical bills.

If you are married with children, you probably are more aware of the value of a good medical plan, but do you know that some companies offer psychiatric and dental coverage as well? How many parents of a troubled teenager would welcome psychiatric coverage! Perhaps you have a child who will need orthodontia work in two or three years. If, among your job offers, is a company that offers no dental plan at all and another that offers all or a percentage of dental costs, you must weigh carefully just how important such a plan is to you.

If you're an "over-forty" person and expect to stay in this job until your retirement, try to find out which offer will give you the most career advancement. One of the firms that has offered you a job may have the levels above your position filled by people your age or younger. But another firm might be able to offer you a position as soon as the immediate supervisor reaches retirement age. How quickly can you get promoted? How high can you go in the company? These, too, are considerations.

Just as job searching is a thinking process, so is job selection. There's much to think about in selecting which job offer to accept. It is never solved by simply flipping a coin. You must try to really think about *you*, decide what is important to *you*, and in which job *you* think *your* skills, talents, and abilities will be used to the most advantage, and where *you* will be the happiest.

And once you make the decision, stick to it, and commit yourself completely. The job-getting is just the first step. The next achievement is in making the job into *your* job. By giving it your all and approaching it with integrity and imagination, you will change your job into a challenging career.

Appendix

Job Descriptions and an Employment Outlook

This information will provide you with the basics on many occupations that are open to you. Besides noting the employment forecast of a field, note that salaries differ in various localities, and at best, can only be approximations because of variations from company to company, differing skill levels within each category, and relative fluidity of the job market at any particular time. A secretary in Napoleon, Ohio, will be earning less than one in New York City, and a newspaper reporter in Chicago or Los Angeles or Dallas will be earning more than one in Dover, New Jersey, or Litchfield, Connecticut, or Somerset, Pennsylvania. This is not discriminatory of the smaller localities, as the cost of living — rent for one thing — is usually lower in a smaller city, and very often jobs in smaller cities are perfect for beginners or people with less experience.

If you are planning to relocate, drop a note to the Chamber of Commerce of that city, and let them know what occupational area interests you. They will let you know the salary range and availability of such jobs. And while you're at it, ask about the availability and rent scales of apartments, too. That will enable you to look at the full picture (in terms of cost of living) in perspective.

Accounting

Forecast

Demand growing.

Education

B.A. or B.S., M.B.A.

Salary Range (annual, entry level)

B.A., B.S.	$13,500–$15,700
M.B.A.	$19,000–$36,000

Advertising*

(Including media, copywriting, marketing, production, research, art and television)

Forecast

Demand growing. However, a highly competitive field.

Education

B.A. or B.S.; M.B.A.

Salary Range (annual, entry level)

Account Supervisors	$30,000–$45,000
Account Executive	$21,000–$30,000
Art Director	$15,000–$25,000
Layout Artist	$ 9,000–$25,000
Copywriter	$20,000–$32,000
Media Director	$16,000–$26,000
Market Research	$14,500–$33,000
Television Director	$19,000–$36,000
Radio/TV Announcers	$ 9,000–$18,000
Photographers	$10,000–$19,000

Computer Science (see Programming)

---

*Position may be attained through secretarial or gal/guy Friday position.

Design

Forecast
Good, especially in large cities.

Education
B.A. or B.F.A. in art, design, architecture.

Salary Range (annual, entry level)

Architects	$16,000–$28,000
Commercial Artists	$ 7,000–$20,000
Display Workers	$10,000–$13,000
Floral Designers	$ 9,000–$14,500
Industrial Designers	$15,000–$20,000
Interior Designers	$12,000–$23,000
Landscape Architects	$13,000–$16,500
Photographers	$10,000–$19,000

Education: Teaching
(Including elementary, secondary, and college)

Forecast
Poor, though there will be an increase in teachers trained in *vocational* areas (plumbing, air-conditioning, television, appliance repair).

Education
M.S. or Ph.D.

Salary Range (annual, entry level)

Elementary		$ 9,000–$14,500
Secondary	*(average)*	$15,000
College	*(average)*	$20,000

Employment Counseling*

Forecast
Employment counselors will have many opportunities, as employment programs are being set up to handle teenagers, dropouts, minorities, handicapped, etc.

Education
B.A., M.S. (personnel, psychology, sociology).

Salary Range (annual, entry level)
$9,000–$21,000

*Position may be attained through secretarial or gal/guy Friday position.

Engineering

(Including aeronautical, chemical, civil, electrical, industrial, mechanical, mining, and nuclear engineering)

Forecast

Steadily growing field. If defense spending increases, there will be a rapid increase in the number of openings.

Education

M.S., Ph.D.

Salary Range *(annual, entry level)*

M.S.

Chemical	to $29,000
Civil	to $20,376
Electrical Engineer	to $22,224
Industrial	to $22,056
Metallurgical	to $28,000

Ph.D.

Chemical	to $35,000
Civil	Open
Electrical Engineer	to $34,000
Industrial	Open
Metallurgical	to $34,500
Petroleum	Open

Government Positions

Forecast

Good.

Education

Ranges from high school through Ph.D.

Salary Range *(annual, entry level)*

High School Level	$10,000–$12,000
College Level	$15,000–$18,000

Health Services

*(Including dental assistants, dental hygienists,
dentists, nurses, physicians, and other technicians)*

Forecast

The entire health field is rapidly growing. Large increases in all
categories of this field are predicted.

Education

Dental Assistants — High school, community college, on the job
training.

Dental Hygienists — *Must be licensed* by the state. B.S., M.S., or
graduate of school of dental hygiene.

Dentists — B.S., D.D.S.

Nurses — *Must be licensed*. Nursing school; college, or community
or junior college.

Physicians — B.S., M.D.

Salary Range *(annual, entry level)*

Aides, Orderlies, Attendants	$ 8,320–$10,660
Chiropractors	*(average)* $30,000
Dental Assistant	$ 9,400–$10,500
Dental Hygienists	*(average)* $13,000
Dental Laboratory Technicians	*(average)* $16,000
Dentists	*(average)* $50,000
Dietitians	$12,600–$30,000
Dispensing Opticians	$11,000–$20,000
Electrocardiograph Technicians	$ 7,800–$15,100
Electroencephalographic Technicians	$ 8,800–$22,600
Emergency Medical Technician	$ 7,000–$19,000
Health Service Administrators	$21,500–$55,000
Licensed Practical Nurses	*(average)* $ 9,000
Medical Assistants	$ 8,700–$14,800
Medical Laboratory Workers	$10,600–$15,300
Medical Record Administrators	$14,500–$30,000
Medical Record Technicians, Clerks	$ 9,400–$16,900
Occupational Therapists	$13,000–$32,000
Occupational Therapy Assistants	$ 9,000–$14,500
Operating Room Technicians	$ 8,600–$15,222
Optometric Assistants	$ 6,200–$13,000

Optometrists	$16,900–$50,000
Osteopathic Physicians	*(average)* $33,000
Pharmacists	$15,900–$33,000
Physical Therapist Aides	$ 6,500–$14,000
Physical Therapists	$13,000–$27,000
Physicians	*(average)* $65,400
Podiatrists	$19,000–$47,000
Registered Nurses	$11,800–$16,800
Respiratory Therapy Workers	$ 9,400–$15,980
Speech Pathologists, Audiologists	$14,300–$28,300
Veterinarians	$18,000–$40,000
X-Ray Technologists	$ 9,400–$14,700

Insurance and Banking

Forecast
Excellent.

Education
Liberal arts (any major) — for sales, underwriting and claims.

Salary Range *(annual, entry level)*

Banking:

Bank Clerks	$ 8,000–$12,500
Management Trainees without M.B.A.	$12,000–$18,000
Management Trainees with M.B.A.	$22,000–$28,000
Bank Tellers	$ 9,000–$11,500

Insurance:

Actuaries	$15,900–$24,500
Adjusters	$11,500–$16,000
Claim Representatives	$13,800–$17,500
Underwriters	$18,600–$28,000

Law

Forecast
Increasing opportunities for high-ranking law graduates.

Education
Law school graduate (LL.B., J.D.)

Salary Range *(annual, entry level)*

Lawyers	$29,000–$40,000
Para-Legals	$16,500–$22,000

Law Enforcement

Forecast
Good for those with college training in law enforcement.

Education
B.A. or B.S.

Salary Range (annual, entry level)
Municipal Officers $12,600–$19,500

Library

Forecast
Poor, especially for schools and public libraries. Slight increase for corporate, medical or technical librarians.

Education
M.L.S. degree.

Salary Range (annual, entry level)
Librarians (M.L.S. degree) $12,500–$16,500
Clerical Assistants $ 8,000–$12,000

Managerial/Administrative*

Forecast

Management may be the fastest-growing occupational field in the country. The continued expansion of management will be steady as industry continues to expand.

Education

College graduate, M.B.A., or a person promoted from a clerical position (typist-clerk, bookkeeper, secretary, etc.)

Salary Range (annual, entry level)

Buyers	$10,300–$26,000
City Managers	$14,000–$42,000
Credit Managers	$ 9,500–$42,000
Hospital Administrators	$12,000–$42,000
Industrial Traffic Managers	$17,000–$42,000
Purchasing Agents	$10,500–$23,900
Urban Planners	$13,000–$32,000

*Position may be attained through secretarial or gal/guy Friday position.

Marketing and Market Research*

Forecast

Excellent opportunities. It's an expanding field.

Education

B.A., B.B.A., B.S.; Ph.D. (psychology, sociology, statistics, mathematics, economics).

Salary Range (annual, entry level)

Marketing Researchers	$13,000–$30,000

Mathematics and Statistics

Forecast

Increasing amount of opportunities.

Education

B.S., M.A., M.S., Ph.D.

Salary Range (annual, entry level)

Mathematicians	$14,800–$30,000
Statisticians	$16,000–$30,000

Newspapers/Magazines

Forecast

Poor. The supply of applicants is much more plentiful than the demand.

Education

B.A. (any major with typing) or M.A. in Journalism.

Salary Range (annual, entry level)

B.A.	$ 9,000–$20,800
M.A.	$15,000–$30,000

---

*Position may be attained through secretarial or gal/guy Friday position.

Office Services

(Including secretaries, gal/guy Fridays, administrative assistants, bookkeeping and word processing)

Forecast

There has always been a profound shortage of trained office personnel. Hence there exist tremendous opportunities for people interested in pursuing secretarial or administrative assistant careers.

Education

High school, business school, or college degree with typing skills. Stenographic skill helpful.

Salary Range (annual, entry level)

Administrative Assistants	$15,000–$22,000
Bookkeeping Workers	$13,000–$15,000
File Clerks	$ 8,000–$11,500
Legal Secretaries	$12,500–$22,000
Office Machine Operators	$ 9,000–$13,000
Receptionists	$ 9,000–$14,000
Secretaries, Stenographers	$14,000–$21,000
Shipping Clerks, Receiving Clerks	$ 9,000–$12,000
Statistical Clerks	$10,000–$14,000
Stock Clerks	$ 7,900–$ 9,300
Typists	$10,500–$15,000

Performing Arts

Forecast

Extremely poor. There have always been more aspirants than parts.

Education

No specific background. Talent and luck are more important than a particular background.

Salary Range

Actors, Actresses (Broadway show)	$400+ *weekly*
Dancers (Broadway show)	$360+ *weekly*
Musicians (with symphonies)	$232–$490 *weekly*
Singers (per performance)	$45–$350

Personnel*

Forecast

This field is growing rapidly as personnel becomes a more complicated procedure (recruiting, Affirmative Action Programs,
wage and salary, benefits, E.E.O., etc.).

Education

B.A., LL.B., M.B.A.

Salary Range (annual, entry level)

College graduate (typing)	$15,000–$20,000
Personnel, Labor Relations Workers — M.B.A.	$17,000–$22,000

Programming

Forecast

Extremely expanding field.

Education

College degree with courses in data processing, accounting, math
or business administration, technical data processing schools,
high school (many offer degrees with training in computer
programming).

Salary Range (annual, entry level)

Computer Operating Personnel	$15,500–$20,000
Computer Programmers	$17,500–$26,300
Systems Analysts	$18,500–$30,000

Public Relations*

Forecast

Expanding field. Companies are more aware of the need to be
known, and this field is the great "information disseminator."

Education

B.A., M.S. (journalism, English, communications, etc.).

Salary Range (annual, entry level)

B.A.	$11,000–$15,000
M.S.	$16,500–$32,000

*Position may be attained through secretarial or gal/guy Friday position.

*Publishing**

Forecast

Good. Although many thought TV would affect America's reading habits, hardcover book publishers, paperback publishers, as well as magazines, report growth in these industries.

Education

B.A. degree.

Salary Range (annual, entry level)

Editorial:

Editorial Assistant	$ 9,000–$12,000
Copy Editor	$13,000–$16,000
Copy Manager	$17,000–$20,000
Assistant Editor	$17,000–$20,000
Associate Editor	$24,000–$30,000
Senior Editor	$24,000–$30,000
Editor-in-Chief	$30,000++

Production/Design:

Artist (graphic)	$15,000–$18,000
Art Director	$18,000–$25,000
Senior Book Designer	$15,000–$22,000
Production Supervisor	$14,000–$23,000
Production Director	$18,000–$40,000+
Inventory/Purchaser	$13,500–$21,500

Sales/Marketing:

Permissions Manager	$18,000–$25,000
Subrights Director	$18,000–$35,000
Publicity Manager	$18,000–$25,000
Library Promotion Manager	$15,500–$25,000
Sales Promotion Manager	$19,500–$30,000
Senior Copywriter	$16,700–$28,000
Direct Mail Manager	$17,000+
College Traveler	$16,000 + bonus
District Sales Manager	$12,000–$28,000
Regional Sales Manager	$15,000–$40,000+
Sales Manager	$20,000–$45,000+

*Position may be attained through secretarial or gal/guy Friday position.

Sales

Forecast

The sales field, like the secretarial field, is recession proof. Job openings always exceed the amount of people pursuing a sales career.

Education

College or high school graduate. (Technical sales usually require a scientific educational background.)

Salary Range (annual, entry level)

Salary/Draw plus Commissions

Insurance Agents, Brokers	$10,800 plus commission
Manufacturers' Salesworkers	$15,400–$38,500
Real Estate Salesworkers, Brokers	$15,000 plus commission
Retail Trade Salesworkers	$ 7,800 plus commission
Securities Salesworkers	$29,000 (includes commission)
Wholesale Trade Salesworkers	$11,000–$27,800 (includes commission)

Sciences

(Including chemistry, physics, biology, geology, and oceanography)

Forecast

The temporary lull in the late 1960s and early 1970s is almost over, and the future in these fields is promising.

Education

M.S., Ph.D.

Salary Range (annual, entry level)

M.S.	$21,000
Ph.D.	$28,000

Social Sciences

Forecast

Of all the social sciences (anthropology, economics, geography, history, political science, psychology), economics is the largest field and anthropology is the smallest. Economics, in fact, is the most rapidly increasing field, with business relying more heavily on it than ever before.

Education

M.A., Ph.D. Less opportunity for bachelor's degrees.

Salary Range *(annual, entry level)*

Anthropologists	$10,700–$30,000
Economists	$12,200–$30,000
Geographers	$10,700–$28,500
Political Scientists	$11,500–$26,200
Psychologists	$13,200–$40,000
Sociologists	$13,400–$26,000

Social Work

Forecast

The demand for qualified social workers is expected to exceed the supply. The forecast is encouraging.

Education

Master's degree in social work (M.S.W.).

Salary Range *(annual, entry level)*

College Career Planning, Placement	$10,500–$22,000
Employment Counselors	$13,000–$21,000
Home Economists	$ 9,000–$19,500
Recreation Workers	$10,500–$22,000
Rehabilitation Counselors	$10,700–$18,500
School Counselors	$11,500–$19,000
Social Service Aides	$ 8,000–$12,000
Social Workers	$10,500–$17,500